American History in No Time

A Quick & Easy Read for the Basics

Randolph G. Russell

Life At

Posterity! You will never know how much it cost the present generation to preserve your freedom! I hope you will make a good use of it. If you do not, I shall repent in Heaven that I ever took half the pains to preserve it.

– John Adams

ISBN-13: 978-1-7333136-7-4

Printed in the United States of America

PREFACE

A line from the hymn "America the Beautiful" reads, "O Beautiful for patriot dream that sees beyond the years." Could those who brought forth this nation in 1776 have imagined that 250 years later, in 2026, nearly 350 million Americans would be celebrating what they did? Perhaps they could. Many of the Founders used the phrase "millions yet unborn" or variations of it to describe the beneficiaries of their work and thus convey its magnitude.

The Founders understood that if liberty was to be preserved, continued effort, vigilance, and education would be required of succeeding generations. Thomas Jefferson said, "If a nation expects to be ignorant and free … it expects what never was and never will be." Our nation's 250th anniversary is a time to reflect on how well we are living up to the high standards our forebears envisioned for us.

- A study by the U.S. Department of Education found that only 12 percent of high school seniors were proficient in American history, far below the results in reading, math, or science.
- In a survey of college students by the American Council of Trustees & Alumni, less than half could identify the rule of law as a core principle of American civic life.
- A survey by the Freedom Forum showed that among the general public, less than one percent of adults could name the five freedoms guaranteed by the First Amendment to the Constitution.

For a self-governing society like the U.S. to function properly, there are certain things citizens need to know. Shared knowledge creates a common bond and a sense of identity. Becoming well informed is hardly a chore, though, because our history is such a fascinating story.

Surprisingly, with all the books that had been published on the subject, no one had written a really concise overview, a quick and easy way to learn the basics every citizen should know. This little book fills that void for young and old alike.

American History in No Time provides a panoramic view of our entire history – the key events, people, places, and principles – from before Columbus to the founding of the United States and all the way up to the present. Divided into brief sections that take less than five minutes each, the whole book can be read in just a few hours.

The book has been used at a number of colleges, but it is easy for anyone to understand, including children and people who may not have liked history before. No matter how old you are, you will be amazed how much you learn with each page.

What does it mean to be an American? It is much more than just being a citizen. The answer lies mostly in our past, and it is now at your fingertips.

CONTENTS

INTRODUCTION

Immediately following this introduction, you will find a timeline of the last 500 years with seven key events already plotted. As you can see, the beginning of Jamestown was as far in the past to our nation's founders as the Civil War is to us. You might want to personalize the timeline by plotting your birth date, the year your parents or grandparents were born, when your ancestors came to America, or the historical events you will soon read about that you find particularly interesting. A map of U.S. territorial expansion and a world map are also provided. More than 200 images are interspersed throughout. Study these pages and refer back to them as you progress through the book to enhance your perspective.

Wherever you live or wherever you go in this country, people have lived there or passed that way for centuries, if not millennia. That realization fosters curiosity about the way things used to be and what the people were like.

One of the purposes of ***American History in No Time*** is to instill a sense of history and a desire to know more. When that happens, you will want to stop at more of the historical markers you see along the roadways. Your vacation to the theme parks in Orlando will include a side trip to St. Augustine, an early colonial outpost of Spain and the oldest permanent settlement founded by Europeans in the continental United States, just two hours away. After visiting the Gateway Arch in St. Louis, you will head 10 miles east to Cahokia and climb to the top of Monks Mound, an ancient Native American earthen pyramid with a larger footprint than any pyramid in Egypt. If you go to the French Quarter in New Orleans for Mardi Gras, you will pause at the corner of St. Louis and Chartres streets, where slaves were auctioned before the Civil War. During your stay in Las Vegas, you will schedule time to see an old mining town nearby called Rhyolite, now a ghost town. And if you travel to New York to take in a show on Broadway or at Madison Square Garden, you will not want to leave the city without walking down Wall Street, the financial center of the country, to stand next to the statue of George Washington, on the spot where he took the oath of office in 1789 as the first president of the United States.

William Faulkner wrote, "The past is never dead. It's not even past." History is all around us if we just look for it. We are connected to the past, and it provides an unlimited supply of incredible stories and valuable life lessons that can make anyone's life much richer and more meaningful. We are moved as we vicariously experience incredible triumphs and heart-rending tragedies. It is inspiring to learn about people who overcame seemingly insurmountable obstacles. We become wiser as we see that circumstances need not define us or determine our future. The goodness we witness from the pages of history prods us to be better ourselves. And when we read about some of the awful things people have done in the past, it can strengthen our determination to eliminate such inclinations in our own character. Connecting with our national heritage imbues us with a deep sense of gratitude for what our forebears did so we can enjoy a better life, and it encourages us to make our own contributions to the country in whatever way we can.

Can we really know who we are if we don't know where we came from? The past helps us better understand ourselves because we see traces of our predecessors in us, and we see in their problems similarities to our own.

Now, the basics.

Declaration of Independence
submitted to the Second Continental Congress

Timeline

1492 Columbus's 1st voyage
1500
1600
1607 Jamestown founded
1700
1776 Declaration of Independence
1800
1861-65 Civil War
1900
1941 Pearl Harbor
2000
2001 9/11 attacks
2026 U.S. 250th anniversary

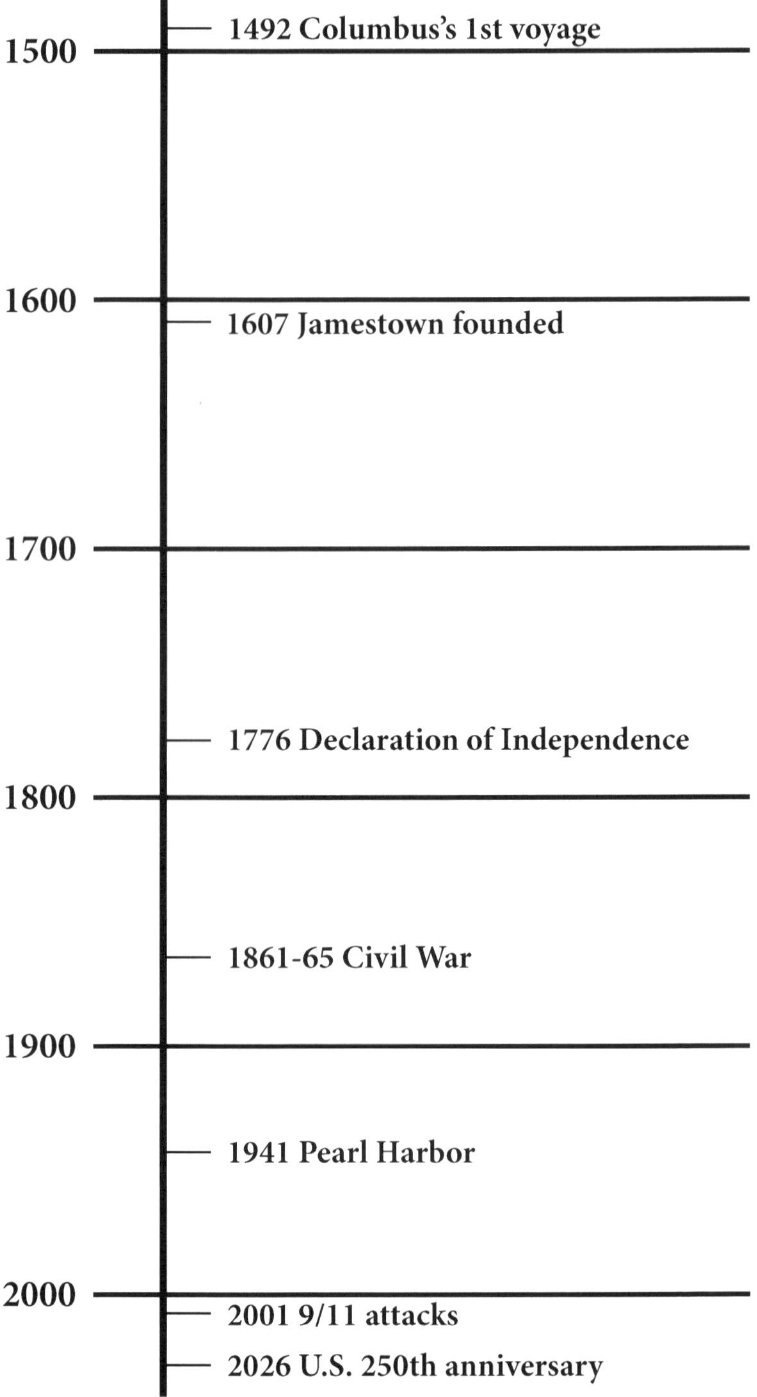

U.S. Territorial Expansion

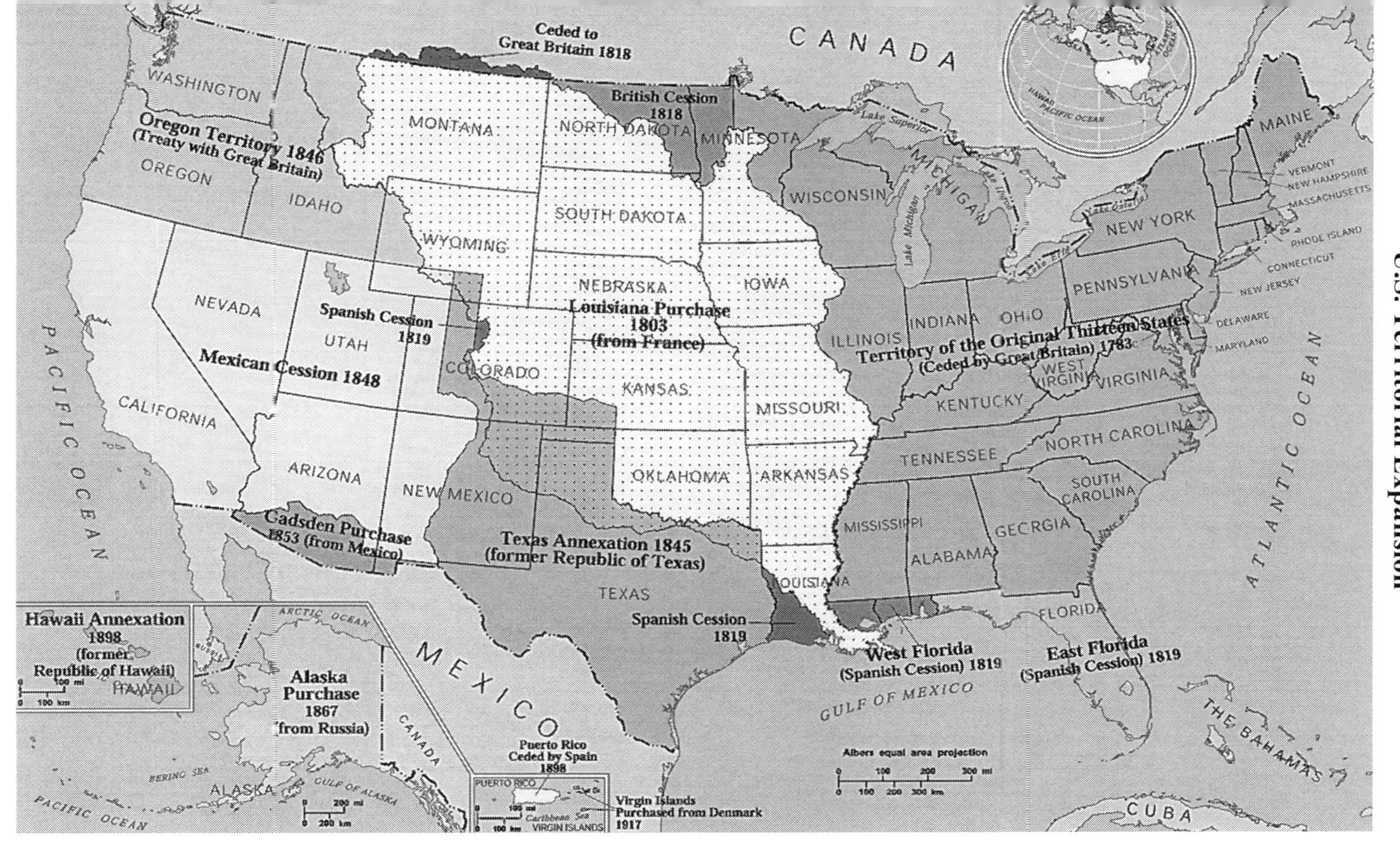

World Map

RUSSIA
MONGOLIA
CHINA
KAZAKHSTAN
INDIA
IRAN
SAUDI ARABIA
TURKEY
UKRAINE
POLAND
EGYPT
SUDAN
LIBYA
CHAD
NIGER
ALGERIA
MALI
ITALY
SPAIN
DEMOCRATIC REPUBLIC OF THE CONGO
ANGOLA
INDONESIA
AUSTRALIA
GREENLAND (DENMARK)
CANADA
UNITED STATES OF AMERICA
MEXICO
ALASKA (USA)
BRAZIL
PERU
BOLIVIA
ARGENTINA

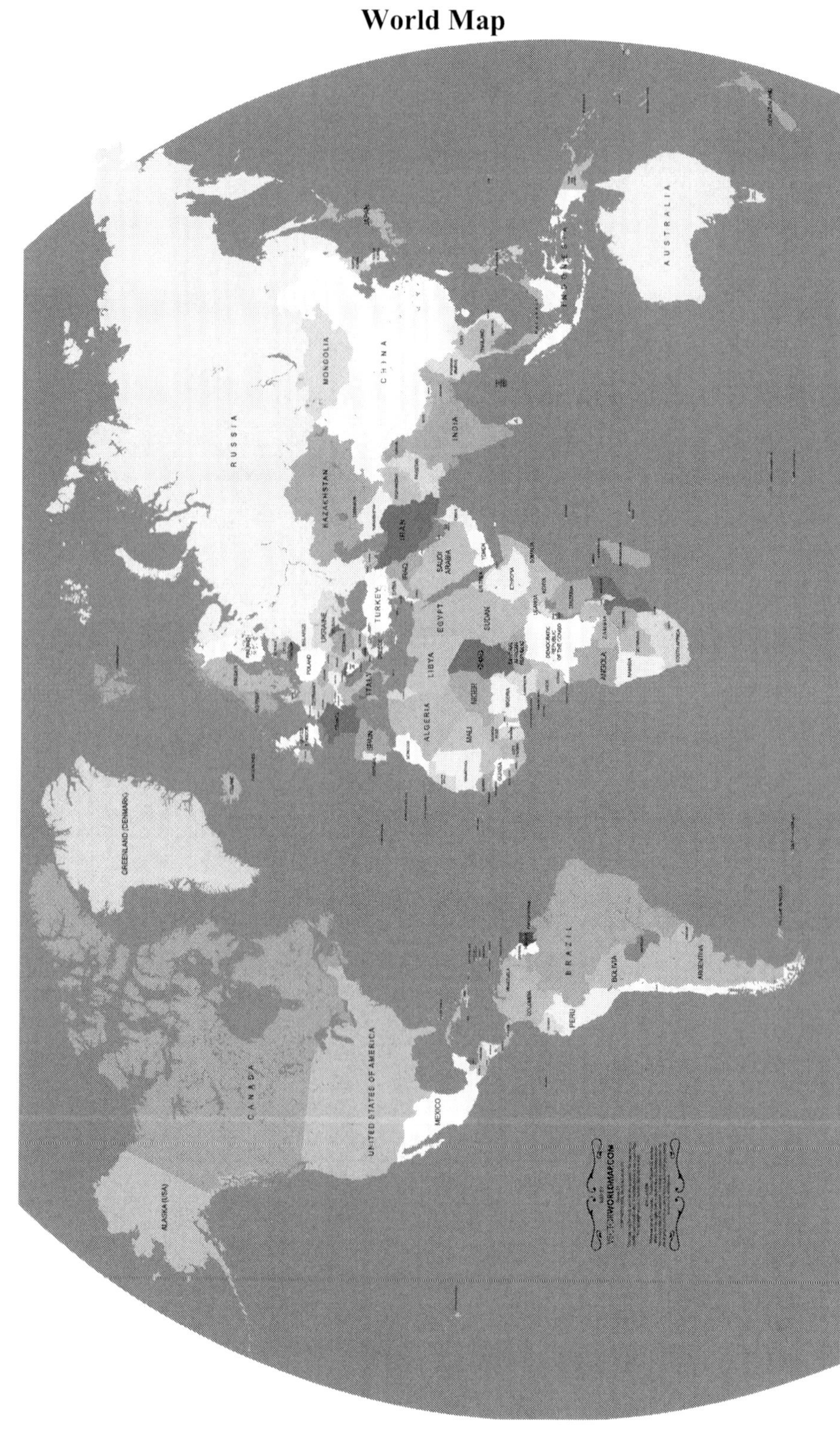

1

ANCIENT AMERICA

Archaeologists do not know how the Western Hemisphere was first populated, but most believe that Asian hunter-gatherers migrated to Alaska across the Bering Strait, possibly a land bridge at the time.* The principal weapon of the earliest inhabitants was the spear.†

American civilization entered a new stage of development with the adoption of agriculture. It began in Mesoamerica, the middle or "meso" region of the hemisphere from Central Mexico to Nicaragua. Three crops grown together rose to prominence as staples – the "Three Sisters," or agricultural trinity of corn (maize), beans, and squash. Other foods native to the hemisphere, including pumpkins, potatoes, avocados, pineapples, tomatoes, peanuts, vanilla, and cocoa, were also cultivated. Early peoples tilled the land without the aid of plows or draft animals.‡

Agriculture provided more predictable, accessible, and plentiful food resources and made settlement possible in more areas. Groups that farmed continued to hunt and gather, however, to supplement their food supply and to obtain pelts and medicinal plants.

Farming started to take hold in what is now the United States around 2000 B.C. It was conducive to permanent settlement but not a prerequisite. In areas where wild food resources were abundant, hunter-gatherer communities were able to thrive.

Ancient Americans did not live isolated from one another. They entered into alliances for warfare and crossed geographic, linguistic, cultural, and tribal boundaries to trade. Copper from the Great Lakes, mica from the Carolinas, turquoise from New Mexico, obsidian from the Rocky Mountains, and shells from the coasts have been unearthed in graves and other archaeological sites hundreds and even thousands of miles away. Indigenous groups also exchanged ideas, language, religious practices, technologies, and labor, and they intermarried.

None of the tribes north of Mexico developed a written language, but linguists have identified more than 300 spoken tongues. Native Americans used sign language to bridge communication barriers. Petroglyphs (images carved into rocks) and pictographs (painted images) were other forms of communication as well as artistic expressions.

* *At the narrowest point of the Bering Strait, only 55 miles separates Alaska and Russia.*

† *The bow and arrow, a more potent weapon, was not in use throughout the present-day United States until 700 A.D.*

‡ *Cattle, horses, donkeys, and plows were all brought to the Americas from the Eastern Hemisphere. Before European contact, the indigenous people of North America domesticated turkeys and dogs. Some dogs pulled sleds and served as pack animals.*

2
INDIGENOUS CULTURES

Native Americans are not a single, homogeneous people. When Europeans arrived in the present-day United States, there were hundreds of tribes within diverse cultures broadly defined by geographic region: the Pacific Coast, the Plateau, the Great Basin, the Southwest, the Great Plains, and the Eastern Woodlands. Their customs, beliefs, languages, survival strategies, political systems, and economies had evolved over millennia.

The abundant natural resources of the **Pacific Coast** supported one of the densest indigenous populations. The diversity of the environment spawned cultural diversity and numerous languages.

Few tribes in the region farmed, even after European contact. They harvested marine life, hunted large and small game in the forests, and gathered seeds, nuts, roots, and berries. Meat and seafood were preserved through drying and smoking. Salmon were a major food source for people in the Pacific Northwest (present-day Washington and Oregon), including the Chinook, Salish, and Makah tribes, who also hunted seals and took whales using large ocean-going dugout canoes.

Acorns (oak nuts), which have to be leached to be edible, were a staple of the Chumash, Ohlone, Pomo, and other California tribes. Their baskets, woven so tightly they could hold water, were used for cooking. Stones heated over a fire were placed in the water along with the food. Constantly stirring the hot stones kept the inside of the basket from scorching while the food cooked.

Round single-family thatched dwellings were typical in California. Tribes in the Pacific Northwest lived in cedar plank lodges usually built to accommodate an extended family. In Washington and areas farther north to Alaska, the people carved and painted the structural beams of their houses with images depicting animals, supernatural beings, family legends, and honored ancestors. The practice was carried over to large free-standing cedar trunks, or totem poles, erected in front of dwellings and at burial sites. Totem poles also served as status symbols.

Another demonstration of social status in the Pacific Northwest was the potlatch. These lavish celebrations marking important family events, such as births and marriages, were also occasions to display one's wealth and distribute it to invited guests. The giving of extravagant gifts enhanced the host family's prestige and obligated recipients of the largesse to reciprocate with potlatches of their own. At some of the gatherings, people destroyed their own possessions as an ostentatious show of affluence.

The **Plateau** region in Idaho, western Montana, and the eastern parts of Washington and Oregon was home to semi-nomadic tribes: the Nez Perce, the Yakama, the Palouse, and others. They hunted bear, deer, and elk and used antlers to dig up wild roots and bulbs, especially camas. To exploit the return of spawning salmon and trout to inland waterways, the indigenous people employed a variety of fishing gear, including nets, weirs, bone hooks, and toxic plants to stun the fish for easy capture.

They built pit houses and grass or wood huts for shelter. Tule mats were used for flooring and additional exterior coverings. Among some Plateau tribes, funerals lasted for days, and mourners burned the home and other possessions of the deceased.

The region known as the **Great Basin** is a predominantly desert environment lying between the Sierra Nevada mountain range and the Rocky Mountains. It comprises most of Nevada and Utah and lesser portions of some of the surrounding states. Rainfall and other water resources vary widely.

The native Ute, Washoe, Shoshone, and Paiute tribes were mobile hunter-gatherers. The most common dwelling was a brush hut stabilized by rocks piled around the outer base. Their food came primarily from plants, with piñon nuts being the staple. Rabbits, antelope, and bighorn sheep provided meat and skins. Well-crafted floatable reed duck decoys lured waterfowl to roost where they could be taken with snares, nets, or arrows.

In the 1500s, Spanish conquistadors ventured northward from Mexico into the American **Southwest**, i.e., present-day New Mexico, Arizona, and parts of neighboring states. They found the inhabitants living in many towns and villages. Spaniards called the natives "Pueblos," the Spanish word for towns. The Hopi and the Zuni were the principal tribes in the region. The Anasazi, Mogollon, and Hohokam were ancestral (predecessor) cultures.

From ancient times, Pueblo peoples relied mainly on agriculture for their subsistence. Through damming and irrigation, hillside terracing, and rainwater collection, they made the most of the available water and were able to produce two crop yields per year on arid land. The irrigation canals dug by those living near rivers were engineered using the topography to best advantage. Some of the canals were up to 25 feet wide and 10 feet deep; the longest stretched for 16 miles.

No indigenous group in the Western Hemisphere used the wheel for transportation prior to European contact. Nevertheless, Pueblo Indians constructed hundreds of miles of exceptionally straight roads as wide as 30 feet in places. Roads fostered interaction and trade between the towns.

Pueblos also traded their turquoise jewelry, decorated baskets and pottery, dyed cotton fabrics, and agricultural goods with people from as far away as Central Mexico and the Pacific Coast.

The most distinctive Pueblo structures were contiguous apartment-like buildings made of stone or adobe* and situated high atop mesas, down on canyon floors, or in large caves in cliff faces. Some of the buildings had multiple levels and hundreds of rooms. Many examples of Pueblo architecture over a thousand years old are still remarkably intact.

Kivas were also prominent features in the towns. These enclosed chambers, usually circular and built below ground, provided spaces for small social and religious gatherings.

Spanish colonization of the American West began in Pueblo territory in 1598 and included the building of Catholic missions to spread Christianity. Spaniards maintained an advantage in mobility by keeping horses out of the hands of the indigenous people, who traveled and hunted on foot.

Hoping to rid themselves of foreign domination, return to their traditional ways, and avenge Spanish abuses, Pueblo Indians in 1680 mounted an attack carefully organized by Po'pay (or Popé), a native religious leader. They killed 400 Spanish colonists along with 21 friars. A thousand survivors of the Pueblo Revolt fled south to El Paso, leaving their livestock behind. Puebloans used the captured horses to barter with tribes from outside the region, and the animal spread across the continent and became an integral part of the broader Native American culture.

A century or two before Spaniards came up from Mexico into the American Southwest, Navajo Indians, enemies of the Pueblos, migrated down from the north and eventually became the largest tribe in the region. Originally a nomadic people, Navajos adopted agriculture and sheepherding and became expert weavers. They dwelt in earthen lodges called hogans but did not establish towns, preferring instead to live as individual families or in family clusters apart from others.

The **Great Plains**, an expanse of prairie with flat grasslands, few forests, and little rainfall, lies between the Rockies and the Mississippi River. Millions of bison (or buffalo) roamed the region. Most tribes on the Great Plains, among these the Sioux, Apache, Cheyenne, Arapaho, Comanche, and Blackfeet (or Blackfoot), followed the movements of the gigantic herds. Flesh from the large animal provided food. Its horns and bones were fashioned into weapons, tools, and ornaments. Clothing, blankets, shelter, and rope came from the hide. The bladder served as a water container, and thread was made from the sinews. Dried bison dung provided fuel for fires.

Nomadic Plains Indians lived in teepees: portable cone-shaped structures framed with wooden poles and covered with tanned buffalo hides. Sedentary Plains tribes, who hunted buffalo only seasonally, lived in grass or earthen shelters.

In the **Eastern Woodlands** between the Mississippi River and the Atlantic Ocean, the indigenous people established permanent settlements prior to adopting agriculture. They subsisted on deer, turkeys, waterfowl, fish, wild rice, tubers, berries, acorns, and hickory nuts.

A trade network operated within the region and as far west as the Rocky Mountains. The birchbark canoe, an ingenious invention so light it could be carried by one person, facilitated travel over inland waterways.

Mounds were a peculiar feature of early Woodlands cultures. Some of the earthen structures served as burial sites or flat-topped platforms for temples and homes of the elite. Other mounds formed geometric shapes and patterns or depicted animals (effigy mounds). Archaeologists have identified more than a thousand of these earthworks built as early as 3500 B.C. during the archaic period, later by the Adena and Hopewell cultures (800 B.C. to 500 A.D.), and finally by the Mississippian culture, which lasted to around 1500 A.D. Artifacts uncovered at these sites – tools, stonework, shell-tempered pottery, hammered metalwork, and jewelry – display a high degree of artistry and technical skill.

The most impressive archaic site is Poverty Point, a regional cultural and trading hub in northeastern Louisiana that was home to hundreds, if not thousands, of hunter-gatherers. Six concentric earthen ridges curve in a semi-circle around a central plaza. The outer ring is three-quarters of a mile in diameter. A massive 70-foot-high ceremonial mound that lies directly behind the rings is believed to have been built in less than 90 days.

The largest single mound yet discovered, Monks Mound, was built 2,500 years later at Cahokia. This major urban center of the Mississippian culture was located 10 miles east of present-day St. Louis, a fertile area near the confluence of the Missouri, Mississippi, and Illinois Rivers. At its peak, Cahokia's population was between 10,000 and 20,000. They manufactured flint tools there.

Monks Mound was constructed over a 200-year period beginning circa 900 A.D. The tiered pyramid contains 22 million cubic feet of dirt, rises in four terraces to a height of 100 feet, and has a base area exceeding 14 acres, a larger footprint than the Pyramid of the Sun in Mexico or the Great Pyramid of Giza in Egypt. The people of Cahokia built 120 smaller mounds within a five-square-mile area.

Half a mile from Monks Mound lies a site that has been called "America's Woodhenge." Cedar posts spaced apart and placed vertically in the ground formed a circle hundreds of feet in diameter. From the vantage point of a single post erected in the center, three of the outer posts aligned with the solstices and equinoxes.

By the time French explorers came upon Cahokia in the 1600s, the city had been abandoned, its inhabitants had dispersed to smaller settlements, and the long tradition of moundbuilding was coming to an end.

Among the many Algonquin-speaking people in the northern Woodlands were the Shawnee, Powhatan, Delaware, Mohican, and Chippewa (or Ojibwa). Wigwams were common dwellings. Branches or felled saplings were fixed in the ground then bent over and lashed together to form a dome-shaped frame, which was covered with bark, hides, or thatching.

Iroquois-speaking tribes in the North included the Mohawk, Seneca, Cayuga, Oneida, Onondaga, and Tuscarora. The traditional Iroquois dwelling was the longhouse, a large rectangular structure that sheltered an extended family. Sheets of bark covered a wood frame typically 20 feet high, 20 feet wide, and 100 feet in length. Smoke from indoor fires escaped through holes built into arched or gabled roofs.

The Iroquois held women in high regard and traced lineage through the maternal line. When a couple married, they lived in the home of the wife's family. Land was held collectively by all the women, and their cultivation of the fields provided the bulk of the food supply. Iroquois women could dictate political actions, such as whether to wage war. The clan mother nominated the male chief, who represented them at tribal councils. She could also depose him.

Among tribes in the southern Woodlands – the Cherokee, Choctaw, Chickasaw, Creek (Muscogee), and Seminole – wattle and daub houses were prevalent. The Indians wove together branches, vines, or strips of wood to form a lattice frame (wattle) that was coated with a mud plaster (daub). Roofs were thatched or shingled with bark.

Estimates of the size of pre-Columbian populations in the Western Hemisphere vary widely. The population north of Mexico, thought to have been between 1 and 15 million, was small relative to the number of people in the entire hemisphere, believed to have been between 8 and 100 million. Whatever the correct figures are, it is generally accepted that European contact led to a dramatic decrease.

Over the centuries, Europeans had built up a natural resistance to smallpox, measles, and other virulent diseases common in the Eastern Hemisphere. Native Americans had no such immunity. When they were exposed, the results were devastating. Millions died. Anthropologists estimate that the indigenous population of North and South America declined by as much as 90 percent in the first hundred years after Europeans arrived.

* *plaster, mortar, or sun-dried bricks made from clay and straw*

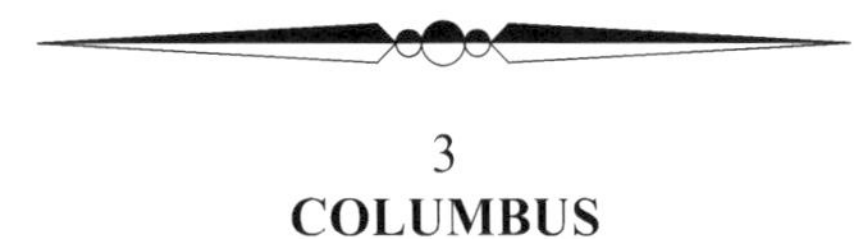

3
COLUMBUS

Silk, cotton, gems, spices, and other goods from South and East Asia (the Indies) were popular in Europe in the 1400s, but transporting them was slow, costly, and dangerous. Trade routes between the two continents were entirely over land or a combination of land and sea. An all-sea route would have significant advantages. Sailing ships could travel day and night and haul heavy loads with relative ease compared to pack animals and wagons. Loading and unloading would be necessary only at the beginning and end of a journey, and bandits and fee-charging middlemen along the existing routes could be bypassed.

While other European explorers pursued an eastward sea route to the Indies around the southern tip of Africa, Christopher Columbus, an Italian, believed sailing west across the Atlantic Ocean would be more direct. For years, he solicited the patronage of European monarchs until King Ferdinand and Queen Isabella of Spain offered their support.

The 40-year-old Columbus set sail from Spain in August of 1492 with a crew of 88 men on three ships: the *Niña (Girl)*, the *Pinta (Painted One)*, and the *Santa Maria (Saint Mary)*, the largest vessel and the flagship on which Columbus sailed. Following a month-long stopover in the Canary Islands, just off the northwest coast of Africa, the expedition headed out over the Atlantic. In the early morning hours of October 12, after five weeks at sea, they sighted a small island and went ashore later that day.

Believing he had reached the Indies and proven his theory, Columbus called the inhabitants "Indians." But he was not in Asia. The ships had landed in the Bahamas, an island chain that was part of the North American continent. The shores of a vast mainland were just 450 miles to the northwest. A second continent lay 800 miles south. Both continents were unknown to Europeans of the day.*

Columbus explored Cuba and other islands in the Caribbean. He claimed the lands for Spain and planted a colony on the island of Hispaniola† before sailing back to Europe. His return after seven months was met with much fanfare. The voyage marked the beginning of the Columbian Exchange: the widespread transfer of plants, animals, ideas, religions, diseases, and people (including the enslaved) between the two hemispheres.

Over the next 11 years, Columbus made three more voyages for Spain, exploring South America and other parts of North America but never setting foot on the present-day U.S. mainland. Notwithstanding his discovery, what Europeans called a New World, Columbus died in 1506 in relative obscurity. Neither continent bears his name.

Amerigo Vespucci was a member of at least two expeditions to the Western Hemisphere after 1492, none of which he commanded. Nevertheless, Vespucci's writings led some to believe that he was the discoverer, and so, the Americas were named after this minor explorer.

* *Around 500 years before the Columbus expedition, the Norse explorer Leif Erikson is thought to have landed in Newfoundland, a large island in eastern Canada.*

† *The countries of Haiti and the Dominican Republic now share the island of Hispaniola.*

4
THE LOST COLONY

Following Spain's lead, other European countries sponsored voyages to the Western Hemisphere and laid claim to territory. English expeditions in 1497 and 1498 led by another Italian explorer, John Cabot, were the basis for England's initial territorial claims in North America, but those claims were not pursued for almost a century.

Colonization of the Americas helped Spain, a Catholic country, become the dominant power in the Western world. English privateers challenged that position by seizing Spanish merchant ships hauling gold, silver, and other commodities from the New World. Sir Walter Raleigh, one of the English mariners or "sea dogs" carrying out the raids, convinced Queen Elizabeth I that a colony in America would be a valuable base of operations to help England compete economically.

In 1587 the English planted a colony on Roanoke, an island midway up the Atlantic coast of North America. They called the region Virginia, in honor of their unmarried monarch, Elizabeth, known as the Virgin Queen.

When a relief ship arrived from England three years later, the Roanoke settlement was deserted. What happened to the Lost Colony remains a mystery. Among the missing 115 settlers was Virginia Dare, the first English child born in the Western Hemisphere.

As a result of the failure, Queen Elizabeth lost interest in colonization across the Atlantic. England's next attempt would come during the reign of her successor, James I.

Pomo cooking basket

Totem pole

Utah petroglyphs

Pueblo cliff dwellings in Colorado

Native American bow hunter

Plains teepees

Blackfoot Indian

Apache bride

Monks Mound

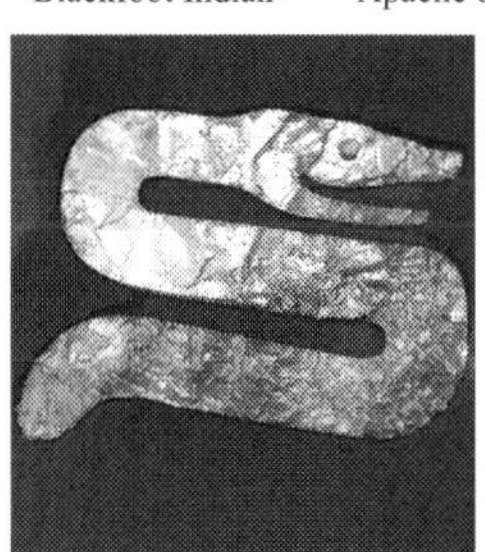
Mica serpent – Hopewell culture

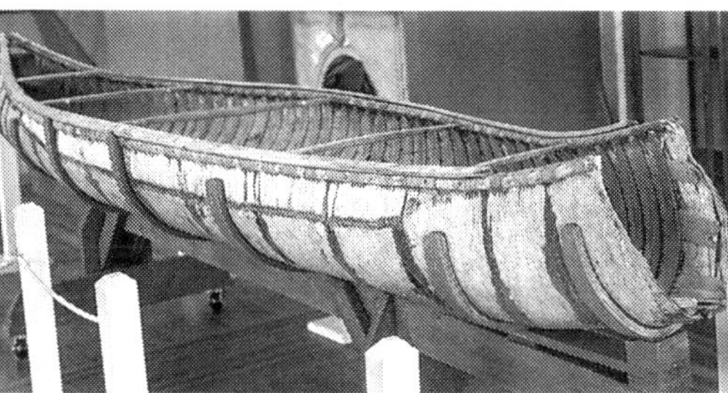
Birchbark canoe

Adena effigy pipe

Knapped arrowhead

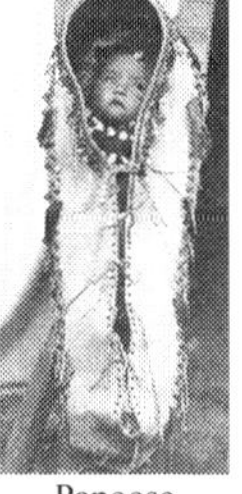
Papoose

Wampum (shell beads)

Interior of reconstructed Iroquois longhouse

Columbus lands in the Bahamas

Spanish fort in St. Augustine, Florida

Captain John Smith

Pocahontas in England

Jamestown church

Mayflower replica

Pilgrims going to church

Old State House in Boston

Trial of Anne Hutchinson

Fraunces Tavern in New York City

William Penn's treaty with Native Americans

Hampton Plantation in South Carolina

5
JAMESTOWN

King James I supported colonizing America to exploit a new source of raw materials, thwart Spanish and French territorial expansion, spread Protestant Christianity, and reduce overpopulation and unemployment in England. In 1606 he granted an English company the right to establish a new colony in Virginia. Investors in the London Company expected to profit from the colony's export of precious metals, forestry products, and agricultural goods, and they hoped colonists would find a "northwest passage," a continuous water route through North America to the Pacific Ocean. Such a corridor to the Orient would give England a distinct economic advantage.

The colony was to operate under a communal arrangement. The company claimed all rights to the land. Colonists would be obligated to work for the company and for the welfare of the group in return for the voyage to America, support after their arrival, and a share of the profits.

Three company ships set sail from England in December with 104 colonists on board, all men. After a four-month voyage via the Canary Islands and the Caribbean, they arrived in the Chesapeake Bay a hundred miles north of Roanoke Island. Sailing up one of the rivers emptying into the bay in search of a place to plant the colony, they chose a peninsula jutting out from the north bank some 50 miles upriver. Water near the shoreline was deep enough to moor their large ships to trees on the bank, which made unloading and loading convenient. Being so far inland from the bay minimized the chance of an attack by marauding Spanish or French warships.

The men named the river and the colony after their king. Jamestown began in May of 1607. Half of the group were gentlemen from upper-class families who were not only unaccustomed to the manual labor necessary to survive in a formidable wilderness, they believed such work was beneath them. The colonists built a triangular fort and a few simple structures inside the one-acre enclosure then wasted time and energy searching for gold, which was scarce in the area.

The decision to settle on that particular site had disastrous consequences. The river was their main source of fresh water, but it was also used to dispose of waste. In the summer, as the water level decreased, so did the river's ability to flush disease organisms downstream. Ocean water pushing farther inland trapped pathogens in the river around Jamestown and added salt to the contamination. Water drawn from the river spread deadly typhoid fever, dysentery, and salt poisoning. Furthermore, the surrounding land, low and marshy, was a breeding ground for malaria-spreading mosquitoes. In the first five months, over half the colonists died, mostly from disease.

The arrival of supplies and more settlers over the next two years, including the first women, helped temporarily, but the newcomers were just as ill-suited to the demands of the colony. Maintaining adequate stores of food was a constant challenge. Company leaders in London failed to recognize the urgency of making Jamestown self-sufficient, and colonists relied too heavily on supply ships from England and trade with the Indians.

Although the company instructed the settlers to take "great care not to offend the naturals," the mere presence of foreigners was enough to spark conflict, especially as local Powhatan tribes realized the English intended to establish a permanent settlement. The Native Americans were willing to trade their surplus food for mirrors, glass beads, copper kettles, and other English goods they found fascinating, but the colonists' persistent demands strained relations. Both sides carried out attacks and reprisals.

After Captain John Smith was elected as Jamestown's fourth leader in a year, he imposed strict discipline, warning: "He that will not work shall not eat." Smith kept the colony in reasonably good condition until he was injured in a gunpowder accident and had to return to England.

During the severe winter after Smith's departure, Indians laid siege to Jamestown, making it dangerous to venture outside the fort for food. Colonists called it "the starving time." They ate snakes, rats, dogs, cats, horsehides, and shoe leather in a struggle to survive. Some even resorted to cannibalizing the dead. When supply ships arrived in the spring of 1610, only 60 colonists were still alive at the fort, although 40 others at an outpost on the bay were healthy. Nevertheless, the commander of the ships deemed the situation hopeless. He loaded up the fort's feeble survivors and set sail for England.

Halfway down the James River, the departing colonists were met by a small boat carrying an advance party of new arrivals from England. They brought word that three large ships were sailing up the river with abundant provisions, 150 settlers, and a governor appointed by the company to take charge. He ordered the Jamestown evacuees to turn back.

The situation slowly improved, and colonists established other settlements nearby. Allocating land for personal use had a dramatic effect. Settlers worked harder and grew more crops on their own private property than they did on communal company land. That, along with the end of a seven-year drought which began in 1606, eventually made food shortages a thing of the past.

In 1614 colonist John Rolfe married Pocahontas, the daughter of the principal tribal chief in the area, after she converted to Christianity. Their marriage brought a temporary peace between the two peoples.

Tobacco, native to the Americas, played a key role in establishing the colony. The leaf smoked by the Powhatans was bitter. Colonists, beginning with John Rolfe, experimented with a mild and fragrant variety of the plant brought up from the Caribbean. It grew well in Virginia, and strong demand in England made tobacco Jamestown's main export,* but tobacco plantations pushing farther into the interior increased tensions with Native Americans.

Representative government was introduced in the Western Hemisphere in 1619 when elected delegates (burgesses) from Jamestown and nearby settlements gathered to make laws for the entire Virginia colony. They called their assembly the House of Burgesses.†

It took time for Jamestown to become secure, and the death toll, one of the worst in the annals of English colonization, remained high for years, but the town survived and took its place in history as the first permanent English settlement in the New World.

As for Pocahontas – in 1616 she, John Rolfe, and their infant son sailed to England, where she was a celebrated visitor, meeting the king and queen. The following year, just as the family was setting out on the return voyage to America, Pocahontas became seriously ill and died. Rolfe buried his 21-year-old wife in England before continuing on to Jamestown.

* *For centuries, tobacco was thought by many to be therapeutic.*

† *Jamestown remained the Virginia colony's seat of government for 80 years. In 1699, Virginians established a new capital six miles away, in Williamsburg.*

6
NEW ENGLAND

The Protestant Reformation in England began in the 1530s with King Henry VIII's rejection of papal authority and the founding of the Church of England, or Anglican Church. Those seeking further reforms faced opposition. The hardships they suffered for their beliefs caused them to look to America as a place where they could practice their faith freely and create a better environment for their children.

The first group to cross the Atlantic for religious freedom had already separated from the Church of England before they left. The Separatists obtained financial backing from a group of London investors who had permission from King James I to establish a colony near the mouth of the Hudson River, a few hundred miles north of Jamestown. The investors recruited others to join the venture who were not members of the Separatist congregation. All 102 colonists would be required to work for the company for a certain length of time under a communal arrangement similar to the early Jamestown plan.

In September of 1620, they set sail from England aboard the *Mayflower*. Unlike the first Jamestown settlers, this group was composed mostly of families. After an eight-week voyage across the northern Atlantic, they arrived in America in present-day Massachusetts, far north of their destination and outside the area granted to their sponsors. Some saw this as an opportunity to strike out on their own, but the Separatists persuaded the other colonists to stick together and work with them to enact "just and equal laws ... for the general good of the colony." Before disembarking, they put their agreement in writing and signed the Mayflower Compact, an important document in America's progression toward self-government.

We refer to this entire group of colonists as the Pilgrims even though only the Separatists made the journey for religious reasons. The colony began at Plymouth, the site of an abandoned Indian village. Finding land already cleared of trees was a great benefit, but the winter was devastating nonetheless. Half their number died from disease and exposure.

Near the beginning of spring, an Indian walked into the settlement and surprised the Pilgrims by greeting them in English. Samoset had picked up bits of the language from English fishermen plying the region's coastal waters. He left Plymouth the next day but returned five days later with a native who spoke English fluently. Squanto (or Tisquantum) had been kidnapped by an English explorer in 1614 and taken to Europe. He made his way back home after five years only to find that disease had decimated his tribe and others. Squanto was invaluable as an interpreter. He showed the colonists how the indigenous people caught fish and eels and cultivated the soil to grow corn, beans, and squash.*

The Pilgrims' leader, John Carver, died in April of 1621. William Bradford, elected to take his place, would lead the Plymouth colony for 30 years. In the fall, the group celebrated its first harvest with recreation and feasting. For three days, Chief Massasoit and a hundred local Wampanoag Indians joined in and contributed five deer to the festivities.†

Working with Native Americans in Maine, the Pilgrims developed a profitable fur trade, particularly in the exporting of beaver pelts. The Plymouth colonists abandoned the idea of a communal economy after just three years.

In 1630 another group left England seeking religious freedom. Unlike the Pilgrims, the Puritans chose to remain members of the Church of England and purify it, albeit from afar. Using a Biblical reference, their leader, John Winthrop, told them their colony in America would be "a city upon a hill" for all to see. They established the Massachusetts Bay Colony in and around Boston, 40 miles north of the Pilgrims in Plymouth. Boston was a better site with a large deepwater harbor and navigable rivers into the interior.

The Massachusetts Bay colonists were wealthier, better educated, and immigrated in greater numbers than their Plymouth or Jamestown counterparts, and their colony progressed more rapidly. They formed a representative government, although participation was limited to male Puritans who adhered to strict standards. Dissent was tolerated but within narrow boundaries. Colonial taxes were used to support the church and establish schools.

The constraints of Puritan society and the need for better farmland compelled some colonists to start settlements elsewhere in Massachusetts and beyond. Roger Williams and later Anne Hutchinson, banished for their beliefs, went south to an area that became part of a new colony: Rhode Island. Thomas Hooker led his congregation to land that became the Connecticut colony. Others moved north to present-day New Hampshire. In general, these breakaway colonies in New England allowed greater religious freedom than Massachusetts Bay, established a clearer separation between religious and political affairs (church and state), and had fewer restrictions on who could vote or hold public office.

* *Squanto was accompanying the Pilgrims on an expedition to trade with Native Americans on Cape Cod in 1622 when he became ill and died. Governor Bradford called his passing "a great loss."*

† *The peace forged by Massasoit and the Pilgrims, although tenuous at times, lasted more than 50 years, but his son, Metacom (called King Philip by the colonists), would wage war against the colonies in 1675-76. During King Philip's War, Native Americans razed 12 of New England's 90 towns, damaged 40 others, destroyed crops, and killed thousands of head of livestock. A thousand colonists and 4,000 Indians died, including women and children on both sides. Indian allies of the colonists helped defeat Metacom, but it was decades before the region fully recovered. Hundreds of captured Indians were sold as slaves and shipped off to the Caribbean.*

7
THIRTEEN COLONIES

England's King Charles I granted Lord Baltimore the authority to establish a colony 200 miles north of Jamestown in 1632. Baltimore wanted his Maryland colony to be a refuge for fellow Catholics, who suffered discrimination at the hands of the Protestant majority in England.

In 1663, Charles II conferred the vast area between Virginia and Florida on eight loyal noblemen. The colony's name, Carolina, was derived from the Latin word for Charles. Carolinians traveled deeper into the interior to trade with Native Americans than any previous English colonists, all the way to the Mississippi River. The colony exported deerskins, cattle, timber, and pine tar (used to caulk ships). Rice and indigo would later become the most important products.

The southern part of the colony had the advantage of an excellent harbor at Charleston. The northern part was rimmed with barrier islands (the Outer Banks) and shoals that were treacherous for ships. In 1712 the colony was split into two separate entities, North Carolina and South Carolina.

Sandwiched between England's northern and southern possessions was a colony of the Netherlands (or Holland), a Dutch-speaking country in Europe. Disregarding Dutch claims to the area, King Charles II bestowed the region on his brother, the duke of York. In 1664 a small English fleet entered the mouth of the Hudson River and landed in New Amsterdam, the main Dutch settlement on Manhattan Island. Unable to muster support to resist the invaders, the unpopular Dutch governor, Peter Stuyvesant, surrendered without a shot being fired. The town and the entire colony were renamed New York.

The duke gave a portion of the territory to two English noblemen. That land became a separate colony named New Jersey.

To satisfy a debt owed to the Penn family in 1681, Charles II granted William Penn proprietary rights to the area between New York and Maryland. Penn, greatly influenced by his Quaker faith, saw his Pennsylvania colony as a "holy experiment" where people of different religions, nationalities, and social and economic classes could live together in harmony. Like Roger Williams of Rhode Island, William Penn respected native cultures and learned to converse with local Indians. He acknowledged their ownership of the land and purchased it from them. He was personally involved in laying out the city of Philadelphia, a name that means "brotherly love" in Greek.

The duke of York increased Penn's holdings with land that became the Delaware colony. Swedes, Finns, and the Dutch had already settled there. Delaware, like all the other colonies except Pennsylvania, had a border on the Atlantic Ocean.

In 1732 King George II issued a royal charter to James Oglethorpe and other trustees to establish the Georgia colony. The following year, Oglethorpe led the first group of settlers from England. Formed from land that had been part of South Carolina, this new colony would assist Carolina in quelling Indian attacks and act as a buffer against the Spanish in Florida, whose outpost at Saint Augustine predated Jamestown.*

Oglethorpe had originally wanted Georgia to be a place where debtors languishing in English prisons could work to pay off their obligations and start a new life in America, but that plan never came to fruition.

The trustees did, however, bring 1,800 poor Englishmen to Georgia and provide them with small farms.

Britain now had 13 colonies in three regions on the East Coast:

New England	Middle	Southern
Massachusetts	New York	Virginia Maryland
Rhode Island	New Jersey	North Carolina
Connecticut	Pennsylvania	South Carolina
New Hampshire	Delaware	Georgia

Each colony had its own set of laws and a governing body with elected representatives and taxing authority, but colonists were still English subjects. The control wielded by Great Britain varied depending on the colony and changed over time.

* *St. Augustine, on Florida's east coast, was founded by Spaniards in 1565.*

8
NO TAXATION WITHOUT REPRESENTATION

As Britain was establishing its colonies along North America's Eastern Seaboard, France laid claim to all the interior territory that drained into the Mississippi River – from the Appalachian Mountains to the Rockies and from Canada down to the Gulf of America (formerly Gulf of Mexico). The claim stemmed from the Frenchman La Salle's 1682 exploration of the river down to its mouth.

Britain disputed part of the French claim in 1754 and sent troops to America. The conflict is called the French and Indian War because various tribes fought alongside the French against the English, who had Indian allies of their own. With support from its colonies, Britain was victorious. In the Treaty of 1763 that formally ended the war, France ceded its territory east of the Mississippi to the British, and Spain, an ally of France, ceded Florida.*

The population of the Thirteen Colonies was now close to two million. They had outgrown Britain's mercantile system, which regarded colonies as existing primarily for the support of the mother country and limited their opportunities for commerce elsewhere. Ninety percent of the colonists lived in rural areas, but Boston, New York, Philadelphia, and Charleston were thriving cities with bustling ports.† The growing economy produced goods for sale within the colonies, to the West Indies,‡ and across the Atlantic, and created a market of American colonial consumers desiring goods from abroad.

After the French and Indian War, Britain exerted greater control over the Thirteen Colonies. The Royal Proclamation of 1763 prohibited colonists from venturing beyond the Appalachian Mountains into the territory recently acquired from France. Then Parliament, the supreme legislative body in Britain, forbade the colonies from issuing new paper money§ and required them to provide food, shelter, and other necessities to British soldiers stationed in America.

The most galling new policy was a stamp tax levied in 1765. Paying off the debts from the war put a strain on the British treasury. To Parliament and the monarchy, it seemed only fair for the colonies to help pay for the support and protection they received from England. The colonial tax applied to printed material. Without a stamp showing that the tax had been paid, legal documents such as deeds and wills would be invalid, advertisements could not be posted, and newspapers, pamphlets, and playing cards could not be sold legally. The tax had to be paid in British sterling, a hard currency that was relatively scarce compared to colonial paper money.

A storm of protest, which included violence, followed the announcement of this first direct tax on colonists. They refused to pay it. The cry in America was "No taxation without representation!" Colonists were not going to accept taxes imposed on them without their own elected colonial representatives in Parliament defending their interests and participating in making the laws. The British government gave in and repealed the Stamp Act the following year but reaffirmed its right to enact laws to govern and tax its colonies.

* *Spain had acquired the French territory west of the Mississippi River in a secret treaty with France in 1762, a year before the end of the war.*

† *The largest cities in America were still small by European standards. In 1760 the population of Philadelphia was 19,000, Boston 16,000, New York 14,000, and Charleston 8,000. London boasted 700,000 residents and Paris 600,000.*

‡ *The islands of the Caribbean were known as the West Indies even though they had no geographic connection with the Indies in Asia (East Indies). Spain, France, the Netherlands, Denmark, and Britain all established colonies in the West Indies.*

§ *The first government in the Western world to issue paper currency was the Massachusetts Bay Colony in 1690. Other American colonies followed suit.*

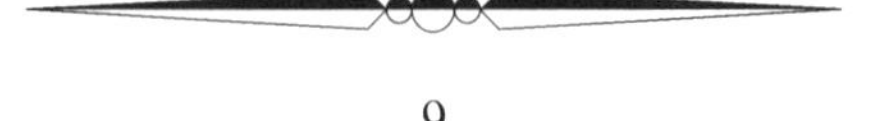

9
MASSACRE and TEA PARTY in BOSTON

In 1767 Parliament passed the Townshend Acts, which levied taxes on English glass, paper, paint, and tea coming into America. Once again, colonists rejected their mother country's authority to tax them without representation. Massachusetts was a hotbed of opposition. Britain dissolved that colony's representative assembly and sent soldiers, nicknamed redcoats, to Boston.*

The night of March 5, 1770, was cold as around 300 people gathered in front of the city's customs house to harass a squad of redcoats. When colonists hurling rocks, snowballs, wood, and chunks of ice knocked one of the soldiers to the ground, the troops fired into the crowd, killing five people. The incident, which became known as the Boston Massacre, ignited a firestorm of protest. The British government tried to calm the situation by repealing most of the taxes imposed by the Townshend Acts but left the tax on tea in place.

In 1773 three English ships loaded with tea sailed into Boston Harbor. The colonial governor of Massachusetts, appointed by the king, demanded that the tea be unloaded and the tax be paid. The colonists balked. In the midst of the standoff, a group of revolutionaries known as the Sons of Liberty, some masquerading as Indians, boarded the ships one evening and dumped all the tea into the water. They were cheered on by thousands of fellow colonists who came out to watch the Boston Tea Party.

Parliament met this blatant act of defiance by passing the Coercive Acts, also called the Intolerable Acts by the colonists. British authorities closed Boston Harbor, banned town meetings,† and extended the boundary of Quebec (a Canadian province also under British rule) south to the Ohio River, thus blocking westward expansion by some of the Thirteen Colonies.

Colonists responded by forming an intercolonial assembly that convened in Philadelphia in September of 1774. Delegates to the First Continental Congress declared the Coercive Acts null and void. They called for a trade boycott against Great Britain and encouraged the people of Massachusetts to take up arms for their defense. The Congress adjourned in October with plans to reconvene in May.

The First Continental Congress demonstrated that the colonies could come together and work out a unified response, but they did not seek independence. Most colonists wanted to remain English citizens. Others insisted that the time had come to break away. In an impassioned speech calling for revolution, Patrick Henry of Virginia declared:

> We must fight! ... Why stand we here idle? ... Is life so dear, or peace so sweet, as to be purchased at the price of chains and slavery? Forbid it, Almighty God! I know not what course others may take; but as for me, give me liberty, or give me death!

* *British troops were an irritating presence in Boston for seven consecutive years leading up to the Revolutionary War.*

† *In the villages typical of New England, town meetings were and still are an example of direct democracy in America. Without intermediaries, residents vote on ordinances to govern their town.*

10
LEXINGTON and CONCORD

With their colonial assembly dissolved and town meetings banned, elected leaders in Massachusetts had to meet secretly. They reorganized the existing militias (civilian military units) and created new ones in preparation for the armed conflict that seemed increasingly likely.* Knowing they would have to react swiftly to stand any chance against the powerful British army, some of the militias trained certain members to be minutemen, patriots who would be ready to fight at a moment's notice.

Colonists kept close tabs on the British soldiers in Boston and devised plans to quickly communicate their movements. If the redcoats deployed at night, patriot spies would use lamps to send a signal from the Old North Church, the tallest building in the city. One lamp would mean the enemy troops were starting out on foot. Two lamps would mean they were being ferried across the harbor before beginning their march.

On a mild spring evening in 1775, the British began preparing boats to transport 700 soldiers. Silently into the darkness the warning went out: two lamps were held up briefly in the belfry of the church steeple.

The rebels sprang into action. They knew the redcoats were heading to Concord, 20 miles away, where colonists had been stockpiling munitions. Paul Revere and William Dawes raced out on horseback, taking different routes to reduce the likelihood that both of them would be apprehended. Church bells, signal guns, beacon fires, drums, and additional messengers on horses alerted the entire countryside that British troops were coming.

Revere and Dawes met up in Lexington, a town along the way, where a young doctor named Samuel Prescott joined them. The three men soon encountered a British patrol, which captured Revere. Dawes and Prescott managed to escape, but Dawes was thrown from his horse. Only Doctor Prescott made it to Concord, but the alarm had been raised far and wide, and colonists were coming out of their homes with gun in hand, ready to fight.

By sunrise, the redcoats had traveled as far as Lexington. Eighty members of the local militia were assembled on the town green, not blocking the road. After the British ordered the militia to disperse, a shot rang out, and both sides exchanged fire. The redcoats killed eight militiamen and wounded nine; one redcoat was wounded. It is not known who fired first, but the militia had orders not to start the fight.

The British army continued on, arriving in Concord later that morning. The colonists had already moved the bulk of their military supplies, but what little the redcoats found, they destroyed. They cut down and burned the town's liberty pole, a rallying spot for anti-British protests.

A brief engagement at Concord's North Bridge left three redcoats and two minutemen dead. Then in the afternoon, as the enemy began their return march, the colonists struck with full force but not head-on. Instead, they fired from behind trees, houses, barns, and fences along the route. The strength of the militias had grown to a few thousand men. The redcoats would have been wiped out or captured had reinforcements not arrived. As it was, they sustained 300 casualties before reaching Boston. American militias lost a hundred patriots that day, April 19, 1775, the beginning of the Revolutionary War.

* *The forming of local militias for protection went back to the earliest days of colonization. Participation was usually mandatory for able-bodied male residents between the ages of 15 and 60, and they were required to use their personal firearms.*

11
SECOND CONTINENTAL CONGRESS and BREED'S HILL

News of the battles at Lexington and Concord spread quickly, and men from across New England gathered around Boston to join the fight. The situation brought a greater sense of urgency to the Continental Congress when, as planned, it reconvened in Philadelphia in May 1775 at the Pennsylvania State House, later called Independence Hall. Delegates to the Second Continental Congress, among the most distinguished leaders in the colonies, laid plans for their defense by creating the Continental Army – a regular army, or one that is permanent and has paid soldiers. The initial recruits would come from the militias already fighting in Massachusetts.* By unanimous vote, the Congress appointed George Washington of Virginia as commander-in-chief of the army.†

Before Washington arrived in Massachusetts, a major battle took place at Charlestown, just across the Charles River from Boston. The engagement is commonly known as the Battle of Bunker Hill even though most of the fighting occurred on the adjacent Breed's Hill, where militias constructed makeshift fortifications of earth and wood. The redcoats began their attack by setting fire to the village, which was providing cover to patriot snipers. The militias repelled two assaults on Breed's Hill but ran out of ammunition on the third and had to retreat. More than a hundred Americans were killed, but the British suffered much heavier casualties and lost many of their officers.

After General Washington assumed command and organized the Continental Army, the enemy holed up in Boston for eight months. To break the stalemate, Washington ordered his men to erect fortifications and place artillery on Dorchester Heights, all in a single evening. From this peninsula overlooking Boston, the Continentals could bombard British troops in the city and British ships in the harbor.‡

At daybreak, the sixth anniversary of the Boston Massacre, the redcoats were astonished to see what the Continental Army had accomplished overnight and quickly realized the precarious position they were now in. The British commander let it be known that they would leave Boston without burning the city if their evacuation was not impeded. American troops held their fire as 8,900 redcoats, 1,200 English women and children, and 1,100 Boston colonists loyal to the crown boarded 120 ships. The fleet set sail for Nova Scotia on March 17, 1776, whereupon victorious soldiers of the Continental Army entered the liberated city.

In less than a year after the war began, the redcoats in Boston, the only British troops in the colonies at the time, were gone. Knowing they would return to America, General Washington started preparing his army for the next battles.

Meanwhile, Thomas Paine, a recent immigrant from England, published *Common Sense*. The 48-page pamphlet was widely read and gave compelling reasons for severing ties with Britain. The Second Continental Congress was struggling to decide whether to take that drastic step, an act of treason punishable by death under British law, or work toward reconciliation. The pamphlet and its popularity helped convince the delegates that a complete break was inevitable.[§] The Congress gave 33-year-old Thomas Jefferson of Virginia, one of its youngest yet most gifted members, the task of writing the document that would announce their decision and give the justification for their actions.

* *Local and state militias would continue to play an important role in the war. They frequently fought alongside Continental Army troops even though they were often unreliable in battle. Their numbers alone were an asset.*

† *Washington refused compensation for his military service.*

‡ *The artillery placed on Dorchester Heights came from Fort Ticonderoga, in upstate New York. The British had given up the fort several months earlier after Ethan Allen, leader of a New England militia, demanded their surrender "in the name of the Great Jehovah and the Continental Congress." General Washington put Colonel Henry Knox, a bookseller by trade, in charge of hauling the 60 tons of equipment to Boston across 300 miles of mountains, lakes, rivers, snow, and mud, a remarkable logistical feat that took six weeks.*

§ *Assessing Thomas Paine's contribution to the Revolution, John Adams said, "Without the pen of Paine, the sword of Washington would have been wielded in vain."*

12
DECLARATION of INDEPENDENCE

On July 4, 1776, the Second Continental Congress adopted the Declaration of Independence as the official announcement of the separation of the Thirteen Colonies from Great Britain and the creation of the

United States of America. Americans have celebrated the Fourth of July as Independence Day ever since. John Hancock of Massachusetts, the leader of the Congress, was the first to sign the original parchment copy of the document. His signature was so prominent and impressive that his name became a synonym for signature. There were 56 signers in all.*

The Declaration set forth founding principles that continue to be a guide and inspiration. It begins:

> When in the Course of human events, it becomes necessary for one people to dissolve the political bands which have connected them with another, and to assume among the powers of the earth, the separate and equal station to which the Laws of Nature and of Nature's God entitle them, a decent respect to the opinions of mankind requires that they should declare the causes which impel them to the separation.
>
> We hold these truths to be self-evident, that all men are created equal, that they are endowed by their Creator with certain unalienable† Rights, that among these are Life, Liberty and the pursuit of Happiness – That to secure these rights, Governments are instituted among Men, deriving their just powers from the consent of the governed – That whenever any Form of Government becomes destructive of these ends, it is the Right of the People to alter or to abolish it, and to institute new Government, laying its foundation on such principles and organizing its powers in such form, as to them shall seem most likely to effect their Safety and Happiness.

Following a list of 27 grievances against the British king, George III, the final paragraph states:

> We, therefore, the Representatives of the United States of America, in General Congress, Assembled, appealing to the Supreme Judge of the world for the rectitude of our intentions, do, in the Name, and by Authority of the good People of these Colonies, solemnly publish and declare, That these United Colonies are, and of Right ought to be Free and Independent States; that they are Absolved from all Allegiance to the British Crown, and that all political connection between them and the State of Great Britain, is and ought to be totally dissolved ... And for the support of this Declaration, with a firm reliance on the protection of divine Providence, we mutually pledge to each other our Lives, our Fortunes and our sacred Honor.

The colonies were now states joined together as a new nation. That system of government, with a central authority and constituent states exercising dual sovereignty delegated to them by the same body of citizens, is known as federalism. The 13 red and white stripes on the American flag represent the original states. The motto *E Pluribus Unum* also expresses the concept of a union of states. This 13-letter Latin phrase appears on U.S. currency and means "out of many, one." ‡

General Washington had the Declaration of Independence read to the Continental Army. He told the men he hoped "that this important event will serve as a fresh incentive to every officer, and soldier, to act with fidelity and courage, as knowing that now the peace and safety of his country depends, under God, solely on the success of our arms."

* *It is not known definitively when all the delegates signed the Declaration.*

† *inherent, natural, intrinsic, sacred (bestowed by God, not people or governments)*

‡ *Congress and President Eisenhower would make "In God We Trust" the official national motto in 1956. That phrase first appeared on U.S. currency in 1864.*

13
COULD AMERICA DEFEAT BRITAIN?

Declaring independence did not make it so. England was not going to give up valuable colonies without a fight. The monarchy and Parliament took action to crush the rebellion.

Americans made the decision to take up arms despite their opponent's considerable advantages. Britain controlled a global empire and was the dominant economic and military power in the world. It could marshal hundreds of ships and tens of thousands of well-trained and well-equipped career soldiers and sailors.

The United States, on the other hand, had only a fledgling navy and had difficulty organizing and maintaining a national army of citizen soldiers.* Americans identified more with their local area and state than with the large nation of which they were now a part. Moreover, the Continental Congress did not have authority to compel men to serve.† Those who did join the Continental Army were often undertrained, poorly armed, and lacked adequate food, clothing, and shelter. Military supplies and financial compensation for the troops were hard to come by without a strong central government.

America was not without strengths, however. Many of its soldiers and commanders had proven themselves in battle during the French and Indian War and in the opening clashes of the Revolution. The war for independence would be fought on terrain more familiar to Americans than the redcoats, and the U.S. would receive support from France, Spain, and Holland. But the biggest advantage for the revolutionaries was that they were fighting for a "glorious cause," namely, their homes, their way of life, and the ideals of liberty, independence, and a new nation.

For some colonists, though, the idea of revolution was abhorrent. They maintained allegiance to England and were labeled loyalists or Tories. The American Revolution was, thus, a war within a war. Patriots had to fight a civil war against armed loyalists at the same time they were contending with the British military.

* *Most soldiers in the Continental Army were between 18 and 25 years of age.*

† *The states sometimes used conscription to fill Continental Army quotas issued by the Continental Congress.*

14
GENERAL WASHINGTON and the CONTINENTAL ARMY

Less than four months after evacuating Boston, the British military returned to America with an intimidating display of power to regain control of the colonies. Hundreds of Royal Navy ships with 32,000 soldiers on board began arriving in New York Bay five days before the Declaration of Independence was adopted.

The Continental Army and state militias, a combined force of 19,000, were nearly overwhelmed in August at the Battle of Long Island. Washington and his men retreated as far as the East River, where they were trapped. A final assault by the redcoats would have probably destroyed the vulnerable rain-soaked American troops and ended the war, but the British commander saw no need to press the attack.

Seizing the opportunity, General Washington rounded up every available sailboat, rowboat, and barge, and under cover of night, quietly directed the ferrying of soldiers, horses, and artillery across the mile-wide river to Manhattan. The direction of the wind aided the American flotilla and kept British ships from sailing upriver to block the escape. The last regiments were still waiting to cross when daylight threatened to expose the ongoing evacuation, but an unusually thick fog rolled in and remained after sunrise, concealing American troops from the enemy's view until all had made it to safety. Washington was the last to leave.

The army was soon retreating again when the redcoats drove the Continentals out of New York and into New Jersey and then into Pennsylvania. The Continental Congress was obliged to relocate from Philadelphia to Baltimore, Maryland. By December of 1776, the Revolution seemed doomed. Most of the soldiers in the Continental Army had enlisted for only 12 months, and those commitments were set to expire on the 31st, at which time the army would likely dissolve. Also discouraging was the seeming indifference of local citizens, state governments, and Congress to the dire supply needs of the army. George Washington wrote to his brother, "I think the game is pretty near up."

In this dark period, Thomas Paine encouraged Americans with a pamphlet series titled *The American Crisis*, which began with the words:

> These are the times that try men's souls. The summer soldier and the sunshine patriot will, in this crisis, shrink from the service of their country; but he that stands it now, deserves the love and thanks of man and woman. Tyranny, like hell, is not easily conquered; yet we have this consolation with us, that the harder the conflict, the more glorious the triumph.

Americans were also inspired by the courage of Nathan Hale, a 21-year-old Yale graduate and a captain in the Continental Army. He volunteered to spy on the enemy but was captured. Right before the redcoats hanged him, he reputedly said, "I only regret that I have but one life to lose for my country."

The outlook was about to change. On December 25, the Continental Army was camped on the Pennsylvania side of the Delaware River. Across the river, Hessian (German) mercenaries fighting for the British held the town of Trenton, New Jersey. The Hessians felt reasonably safe. Not only was it Christmas, but the weather was bitterly cold and stormy, snow covered the ground, and floating ice in the river all made an attack by the Americans seem highly unlikely.

That night, the Continental Army quietly crossed the Delaware in boats and barges and made its way to Trenton. The call-and-response password Washington gave the men to identify the enemy or each other in the dark was "Victory – or Death." By daybreak, the Continentals had reached the town undetected. They got into position and opened fire. In a total rout lasting only an hour, a hundred Hessians were killed or wounded and 800 were taken prisoner without one American battle death. Elated that his bold and desperate gamble had paid off, the commander-in-chief exclaimed, "This is a glorious day for our country."

But there was still the problem of expiring enlistments. The British would soon launch a counterattack, and there would be no army to meet them. On December 30, General Washington pleaded with his soldiers to stay a little longer even though they were cold, ragged, hungry, and exhausted. He told the men, "We know not how to spare you." Most of them remained. Later that week, he successfully led them against British regular troops at Assunpink Creek (also called the Second Battle of Trenton) and then at Princeton. These three stunning victories in New Jersey, all coming within a 10-day period, turned the tide of the war and boosted American morale. New recruits swelled the ranks of the Continental Army and were willing to enlist for the long term, either three years or the duration of the war.

Concord's North Bridge

Minuteman statue

Thomas Paine

Thomas Jefferson

John Adams

IN CONGRESS, JULY 4, 1776.

The unanimous Declaration of the thirteen united States of America,

Declaration of Independence

Benjamin Franklin

General George Washington

Washington leads the Continental Army across the Delaware River toward Trenton

March to Valley Forge

Von Steuben drilling the troops

British surrender at Yorktown

James Madison

Alexander Hamilton

Constitutional Convention

We the People of the United States,

Preamble to the Constitution

Capitol

White House

Supreme Court

Voting booths, where the voice of the people is manifested

Arlington National Cemetery

15
VALLEY FORGE and SARATOGA

Early in 1777, General Washington inoculated his troops against the smallpox epidemic (1775-1782), which was spreading across the U.S. and affecting recruitment and the military readiness of the army.

In July, 15,000 redcoats sailed out of New York bound for the Chesapeake Bay. After disembarking in Maryland, they marched toward Philadelphia. When the Continental Army failed to stop them at the Battle of Brandywine, members of Congress had to flee the city again. Following another defeat, at nearby Germantown, the commander-in-chief led 14,000 troops to Valley Forge to take up winter quarters.

The Valley Forge encampment, just 20 miles from the British army occupying Philadelphia, stretched for three miles along the Schuylkill River. It would be the Continental Army's base for the next six months, through both winter and spring. Washington had the soldiers construct 1,700 small log cabins for their lodging. The simple structures provided a modicum of comfort, but the conditions were still harsh. Food, clothing, blankets, and shoes were in short supply, and illness was widespread. Around 1,800 soldiers died.* Washington pressed the Continental Congress and the state governments for assistance in providing for his men. Aid of a different sort came from an unlikely source.

Friedrich von Steuben, a former officer in the Prussian military, traveled to Valley Forge and volunteered to help train the Continental Army. He was appalled by what he saw and said that no European army would have held together under such conditions. General Washington gladly accepted his assistance. Von Steuben did not speak English. His native language was German, but he also spoke French, as did some members of Washington's staff. The translation of von Steuben's profanity-laced instructions from French to English was often comical to the troops, but he transformed them into a disciplined fighting force by producing a detailed training manual and teaching the essentials of military drill using a model unit of 100 soldiers to help train the rest of the army. His insistence on proper sanitation was also invaluable.

Amid the hardships, troops at Valley Forge were encouraged by the far-reaching effects of a key battle won by other patriots 300 miles to the north. The British had launched an offensive out of Canada to cut off New England from the other states. The redcoats recaptured Fort Ticonderoga, but their advance stalled due to supply problems and a numerical disadvantage against American regular troops and militias. British General John Burgoyne and the 6,000 men under his command surrendered in October 1777 at Saratoga, New York.

The defeat of such a large army raised the hopes of Americans more than any previous victory. It secured the northern states against British attacks out of Canada, but more important, it convinced the French that their centuries-old foe, the British, could be defeated by the U.S. After the Battle of Saratoga, France officially entered the war as America's ally. In addition to the money and munitions they were already supplying, the French would now also provide soldiers and naval support.

* *Conditions at the encampment in Morristown, New Jersey, in 1779-80 were even worse, although there were fewer deaths. It was one of the harshest winters in recorded history, which exacerbated already chronic supply problems. During one particularly bad period, the soldiers were left with nothing to eat for days, and in desperation they chewed on pieces of tree bark just to have something in their mouths.*

16
YORKTOWN

With the war at a stalemate in the Northern states, the British embarked on a major military campaign in the South in late 1778, drawing support from loyalists in the region.* It went badly for Americans early on. After Savannah, Georgia, fell to the redcoats, the U.S. suffered its worst defeat of the war when 5,500 troops surrendered another port city: Charleston, South Carolina.

The United States narrowly averted a disaster in New York. General Washington had appointed Benedict Arnold as commander of West Point, a strategic U.S. fort on the Hudson River. The fort's formidable defenses were engineered by Polish patriot Thaddeus Kosciuszko. Arnold, a hero of the Battle of Saratoga, made plans to hand over the fort to the redcoats for a large sum of money. Three militiamen foiled the plot by catching Arnold's British accomplice with documents related to the conspiracy hidden under his clothing. The Continental Army hanged the spy, but Benedict Arnold escaped to the enemy occupying New York City before he could be arrested. Given the rank of general in the British army, he was soon fighting against his former countrymen. His name became synonymous with treason and betrayal.

The state of affairs in the South improved in 1780 with Washington's appointment of Nathanael Greene as commander of the region. After part of his forces led by Daniel Morgan scored a brilliant victory at the Battle of Cowpens in the South Carolina backcountry, General Greene kept outmaneuvering the enemy and eroding their strength until the redcoats moved northward out of the Carolinas. The British commander in the South, Charles Cornwallis, established his base of operations at Yorktown, Virginia, on the banks of the York River, and unwittingly set the stage for a decisive battle.

General Washington was planning to attack the British stronghold of New York City when he learned that Cornwallis was at Yorktown and the French fleet commanded by Admiral de Grasse was sailing up from the Caribbean toward Virginia. Washington quickly mobilized both

U.S. and French forces to converge on Yorktown. British ships set sail from New York to evacuate Cornwallis and his army. Victory largely depended on which ships arrived first. Fortunately, they were French.

The French fleet blocked the Royal Navy from rescuing Cornwallis by sea. American and French troops led by Washington, von Steuben, and the French commanders Rochambeau and Lafayette sealed off overland escape routes. With nowhere to turn, General Cornwallis and the 8,000 troops he commanded laid down their arms on October 19, 1781, after a month-long siege. Their defeat convinced Great Britain that the war was lost.

* *To punish patriot slaveholders, the British offered freedom to their slaves but not to those belonging to loyalists. Thousands of slaves escaped to safety with the redcoats and lived as free people outside the U.S. When the war ended, escapees in British custody who had not yet left America were handed over to their former slave masters.*

17
TREATY of PARIS and ARTICLES of CONFEDERATION

Fighting continued sporadically for two years after the Battle of Yorktown as British troops and loyalists left the U.S. and diplomats worked out a peace treaty in France. The Treaty of Paris negotiated by Benjamin Franklin, John Adams, and John Jay formally ended the Revolutionary War in 1783. Britain ceded all of its territory south of Canada between the Atlantic Ocean and the Mississippi River. The young nation celebrated as the last redcoats sailed out of New York City on November 25, and General Washington and soldiers of the Continental Army entered.

In the midst of the euphoria, Washington was arguably the most powerful person in the country, but he had no inclination to use that status to assume political power. After bidding an emotional farewell to his troops and his officers, he promptly traveled to Annapolis, Maryland, where Congress was meeting, and resigned his commission as commander-in-chief. This act demonstrated his conviction that the military was subordinate to civil authority. A private citizen once again, the 51-year-old retired general mounted his horse and headed for Mount Vernon, his Virginia estate 45 miles away, arriving in time to spend Christmas at home for the first time in eight long years.

With the old British government thrown off, the United States could now concentrate on setting up enduring American government institutions. This was much easier at the state level because states were largely autonomous, and their predecessor colonial governments had long histories. At the national level, the Continental Congress had been a provisional government concerned primarily with prosecuting the war. The first attempt at establishing something permanent was the

Articles of Confederation, ratified by the last of the 13 states in 1781, more than three years after the first state had approved the document. The government thus created had just one main body: Congress.

The Confederation Congress oversaw the successful conclusion of the war and a peace treaty with Britain. It made substantial progress toward settling the nation's debts, established various government departments (war, foreign affairs, finance, post office), and built up a staff of managers, secretaries, clerks, and translators to handle the day-to-day tasks, including during times when Congress was not in session. The government also formulated guidelines for the survey, sale, and governance of U.S. land between the original 13 states and the Mississippi River. Instead of simply extending the existing state boundaries westward, new states would be formed out of the territory after certain criteria were met.

On the whole, though, the government created by the Articles proved inadequate. It was weak by design. The Founders feared that a strong government would take away the liberties they had fought to secure, but they were too cautious. The Articles did not give the central government authority to enforce its measures. It had to rely on the goodwill of the states. Consequently, laws enacted by the Confederation Congress were little more than recommendations.

This led to many problems, not the least of which was the raising of revenue. Taxation was the purview of state and local governments. The Articles granted the federal government no such authority. The expenses of Congress and the country's debts from the war were to be paid out of a treasury funded by the states, but states could not be forced to pay their share, and their payments were delinquent. A central government without sufficient, timely, and independent funding could not be effective.

Under the Articles of Confederation, the government had little power to regulate domestic or foreign trade. Congress entered into treaties of commerce with other countries but could not compel the states to abide by the provisions. States imposed their own taxes and restrictions on foreign trade as well as interstate commerce, including on goods just passing through to other states. The nation did not have a stable and uniform monetary system. Seven states issued their own currency.

The Articles had additional flaws. Each state was allotted one vote on legislation considered by the Congress. This gave states with small populations as much power in the government as large states. Legislation on such important matters as raising a military force, entering into treaties, borrowing money, and making expenditures required a two-thirds vote rather than a simple majority. A unanimous vote was required to amend the Articles. Congress could not override a state law.

Members of Congress served one-year terms up to a maximum of three terms in a six-year period, which created a problem of continuity in the government. Compounding matters, delegates often showed their state's indifference toward the institution by staying home instead of attending congressional sessions.

The Confederation Congress failed to persuade or coerce Spain to grant Americans unfettered navigation of the Mississippi River. It was also unable to get Britain to evacuate its outposts on U.S. soil along the Canadian border, a stipulation of the Treaty of Paris.

In 1786, only three years after the end of the Revolutionary War, an armed uprising broke out in Massachusetts over high taxes. The rebels took over courthouses to prevent judges from ordering the seizure of their property to satisfy unpaid assessments. Twelve hundred disaffected citizens led by Daniel Shays threatened a federal arsenal. The state appealed to the central government for assistance, but Congress lacked the wherewithal to help.

A former officer in the Continental Army suggested to George Washington that he use his influence to help put down the insurrection. Mortified by this violent challenge to law and order, Washington replied, "Influence is no government. Let us have one by which our lives, liberties, and properties will be secured."

Foreign nations, especially Great Britain, expected the United States to collapse. The civil unrest in Massachusetts and other states was seen as proof that Americans were incapable of governing themselves. A state militia funded by Massachusetts merchants finally quelled Shays's Rebellion in February of 1787, but the inability of the Confederation Congress to deal with the crisis underscored the desperate need for a stronger central government and a more effective framework.

18
THE CONSTITUTION

To address the defects in the Articles of Confederation, a convention was planned to begin in May 1787 in Philadelphia. George Washington's decision to attend added to the prestige of the gathering and attracted other prominent and able men. It was "an assembly of demigods" according to Thomas Jefferson, who was serving abroad as ambassador to France. Every state but Rhode Island sent representatives.

Members of the Constitutional Convention, meeting in Independence Hall where the Declaration was adopted, realized the enormity of their task and what was at stake. Virginia delegate George Mason wrote, "The revolt from Great Britain and the formations of our new governments at that time were nothing compared to the great business now before us." He believed their work would lead to "the happiness or misery of millions yet unborn."

The first order of business was to select someone to preside over the proceedings. Delegates chose the widely respected George Washington. They then agreed to keep their deliberations strictly confidential until their work was completed. This would encourage open and frank discussion of the issues and make it easier for members to change positions. Had the meetings been open to the public or the press, or if the participants had divulged information to outside parties, it is doubtful that the Constitutional Convention would have succeeded.

From the outset, there was general agreement that the central government had to be stronger. The debate revolved around three fundamental questions:

- How powerful should the federal government be?
- How should it be structured?
- How should each state be represented?

Instead of merely revising the Articles of Confederation, as Congress and the states had instructed, these Founders set about creating a completely new document and a truly national government. James Madison is called the "father of the Constitution" because he was the driving force behind the convention and the Virginia Plan, the starting point or basis for debate.

The issues were complicated, and the delegates represented diverse interests and constituencies. They had to compromise for the process to be fair and to reach a consensus. Working every day except Sunday, they debated the important matters and resolved differences. On some points there were sharp disagreements. There were days when the convention seemed destined for failure, but the delegates persisted.

After four months of meetings, they agreed on a final draft written primarily by Pennsylvania delegate Gouverneur Morris. On Monday, September 17, 1787, the convention convened for the last time to sign the Constitution. Washington went first; thirty-eight others came forward by state. Their average age was 44. A third of the men were in their twenties and thirties. At 81, Benjamin Franklin of Pennsylvania was by far the oldest framer of the Constitution.

In only four pages, the document laid out a new form of government. The Preamble states the purpose:

> **WE THE PEOPLE** of the United States, in Order to form a more perfect Union, establish Justice, insure domestic Tranquility, provide for the common defence, promote the general Welfare, and secure the Blessings of Liberty to ourselves and our Posterity, do ordain and establish this Constitution for the United States of America.

The signing in Philadelphia did not make the document the law of the land. As specified by the last of its seven articles, the Constitution would have to be approved by the states, but not by their respective legislatures. Instead, delegates chosen by the people would decide the matter in special state conventions. Mindful of the difficulty in reaching unanimity, the Framers stipulated that the Constitution would become binding upon all ratifying states when two-thirds of the state conventions voted in favor. Approval had to be unconditional; no amendments were allowed before ratification.

After receiving the document, the Confederation Congress forwarded copies to the states for consideration. The outcome was not at all certain. In a series of 85 essays – known collectively as *The Federalist Papers* – Alexander Hamilton of New York, James Madison of Virginia, and John Jay of New York explained the proposed Constitution and made compelling arguments for its ratification.

In December, Delaware was the first state to vote in favor. One by one, the other states followed. In June 1788, New Hampshire became the ninth state to vote for ratification. Having reached the ⅔ threshold, the Constitution became law. By 1790 all 13 states had ratified it.

The Constitution is the supreme law of the land. No federal statute may contradict it. The Constitution, federal laws and regulations, and U.S. treaties take precedence over conflicting state provisions.

The Constitution guarantees to every state a republican (representative) form of government and protection from invasion and domestic violence. Citizens are entitled to the same "privileges and immunities" in all the states but may not flee from one state to another to escape criminal prosecution. States may not issue money or enter into treaties with foreign countries and are required to recognize the acts of the other states (give "full faith and credit"). The Constitution forbids a religious test for holding federal office, bars the taxing of a state's exports, and permits the use of the military to enforce federal law and suppress insurrections.

19
THREE BRANCHES

The Constitution laid out a brilliant structure for the national government, limited in its jurisdiction over states and citizens but strong enough to be effective. Though a creation of the states, the federal government is, within the limits specified by the Constitution, a higher power than any state government or group of states. The government's power, derived "from the consent of the governed," is divided among three branches.

The first and lengthiest article of the Constitution is devoted to the ***LEGISLATIVE BRANCH***, or Congress, the predominant* and most representative branch of the government. Congress writes the laws, including those controlling federal revenues and expenditures. The legislature is empowered to raise an army and navy, declare war, levy taxes, borrow money, coin (or print) money, and regulate commerce in the United States and with foreign nations.

Congress is bicameral with a House of Representatives and a Senate. Representation in these two chambers was one of the most divisive issues at the Constitutional Convention. Large states, such as Virginia, favored population as the basis for representation. New Jersey and other small states lobbied for equal representation, a continuation of the Articles of Confederation model. The agreement that overcame the impasse has been called the "Great Compromise." State representation would be equal in the Senate and by population in the House.

To achieve proportional representation in the House of Representatives, the country is divided into congressional districts within each state. Each district, roughly the same size in terms of population, has one member in the House.† States with larger populations have more congressional districts. California, the most populous state, currently has 52 congressional districts and, therefore, 52 seats in the House of Representatives. Delaware, Alaska, and four other states with relatively small populations have only one congressional district and one representative each. All House seats come up for re-election every two years.‡

Since state populations fluctuate, the Constitution requires the government to take a census, or count, of the country's population every 10 years. States with large population increases relative to the other states gain one or more seats in the House of Representatives while states with large population decreases lose seats. When a state's apportionment changes, say from four congressional districts to five, or when sizeable demographic shifts occur within a state, the district boundaries within that state have to be redrawn, which is supposed to be done in an equitable manner without partiality toward certain constituencies ("gerrymandering"). In most states, governors and state legislators have the primary responsibility for redistricting, but the new boundaries are subject to judicial review if someone files a lawsuit challenging the changes.

In the Senate, representation is equal. Every state, regardless of its size in land area or population, has two senators. Each represents the entire state. Senators are elected for six-year terms, but they do not all face re-election in the same year. Every two years, a third of the Senate comes up for re-election. Likewise, the senators of a state do not both face re-election in the same year (except in special elections). Staggering senatorial elections in this manner promotes continuity in the Congress.§

Revenue (tax) bills must originate in the House of Representatives, but other legislation may be initiated by either chamber. A quorum (a majority of a chamber's members) must be present before a bill can be put to a vote. Most legislation passes with a simple majority of those present voting in favor.¶ The vice president may cast a tie-breaking vote in the Senate.

If the House and Senate pass different versions of a bill and compromise is possible, members from both chambers try to work out the differences in a conference committee. Compromise bills must be put to a vote. Only after an identical bill passes in both the House and the Senate does legislation move on to the White House for approval.

The ***EXECUTIVE BRANCH***, described in Article II of the Constitution, is headed by a single president who, along with a vice president, is elected every four years and represents all the people in the country. The president has to be at least 35 years old and must be a natural-born citizen.# The highest official in the government, he exercises powers set forth by the Constitution and Congress and is charged with enforcing federal laws. The president approves or rejects bills passed by the legislature and may also recommend legislation. He makes treaties with foreign countries, appoints ambassadors and federal judges, and is commander-in-chief of the military.

The president chooses a cabinet to help run the executive branch. Cabinet members manage various departments and are all given the title of secretary except for the head of the Justice Department, whose title is attorney general. There are currently 15 cabinet-level executive departments: War (or Defense), State (foreign affairs), Treasury, Justice, Interior, Agriculture, Commerce, Labor, Health & Human Services, Housing & Urban Development, Transportation, Energy, Education, Veterans Affairs, and Homeland Security.

The third branch of the central government, the ***JUDICIAL BRANCH***, consists of the federal courts. The jurisdiction of these courts, or their authority to hear a case, is defined by Article III of the Constitution and by federal statute. Federal courts handle cases involving the Constitution, federal laws and regulations, and treaties. They also take up controversies between the states, between citizens of different states, and between American citizens and foreigners.

The judicial branch has three main levels: district courts, circuit courts (also called courts of appeals), and the Supreme Court (also called the high court). The Constitution created the Supreme Court and authorized the legislative branch to create the lower federal courts. Congress determines the number of judges at all levels of the federal judiciary.

Judicial Level	Number of Courts	Number of Judgeships
District Court	94	677
Circuit Court (Court of Appeals)	13	179
Supreme Court	1	9

U.S. district courts are trial courts and courts of original jurisdiction, meaning they hear cases at their inception.▲ Every state has at least one federal district court; the most populous states have four. In district court cases, verdicts are rendered either by judges or by juries. At all other levels in the federal court system, only judges decide cases.

If warranted, parties in a district court case may appeal the court's ruling to the regional circuit court. For example, the 7th Circuit hears appeals from district courts in Illinois, Indiana, and Wisconsin. A circuit court decision may be appealed to the highest federal court, the Supreme Court.

Federal judges are not elected. They are nominated by the president and, with the "advice and consent" of the Senate, appointed for life, if they choose to serve that long. Nominees must be confirmed by the Senate before they can sit on the bench.

Courts do not initiate lawsuits. They interpret and apply the law in adjudicating cases brought before them. Rulings by the judiciary frequently rely on precedent, how relevant cases were decided in the past.

States have their own constitutions and governments that mirror the structure of the federal government.◊ Executive, legislative, and judicial branches at the state level operate in their jurisdictions in a similar manner to their counterparts at the national level. There are state senators, state representatives, and state judges. The chief executive of a state carries the title of governor. State and local courts handle most legal disputes in the country.

* *Congress is the only branch that can initiate legislation or remove members of the other two branches. In* The Federalist Papers (No. 78)*, Alexander Hamilton explained why the judiciary is the weakest branch. The three branches of the federal government have different functions and, therefore, are separate, not equal.*

† *Originally there was one representative for every 30,000 residents. The average congressional district population after the 2020 census apportionment was 761,169.*

‡ *An act of Congress signed by President William Howard Taft in 1911 capped the size of the House of Representatives at 435 members.*

§ *State legislatures used to choose U.S. senators. Since ratification of the 17th Amendment in 1913, citizens in each state have elected their senators by direct vote.*

¶ *Senate rules allow for filibustering, a parliamentary procedure that prolongs debate to prevent a bill from coming to a vote. It takes at least 60 senators (⅗ of the total 100) to end debate (invoke cloture) and allow voting to proceed. Thus, 41 senators can block legislation favored by the majority. House rules do not permit filibusters.*

"Natural-born" is generally accepted to mean born on U.S. soil. Whether it also means being born to parents who were citizens or legal residents is less certain.

▲ *The Supreme Court has original jurisdiction over a small range of cases, including those involving ambassadors and lawsuits in which a state is a party.*

◊ *Unlike the U.S. Congress, both chambers of state legislatures are apportioned by population, but state house districts are smaller than senate districts, so there are more state representatives than senators. (See 1964 Supreme Court case* Reynolds v. Sims) *Nebraska is the only state with a unicameral legislature.*

State legislators are paid much less than their counterparts in the U.S. Congress, and in most states, the position is not considered a full-time job. Compensation varies by state, and many state legislators also have private sector jobs to support themselves.

20
CHECKS and BALANCES

The framers of the Constitution limited the power of the federal government by assigning its major functions – legislative, executive, and judicial – to three separate branches. Checks and balances built into the Constitution safeguard this separation of powers by giving each branch a degree of leverage over the other two. These provisions were formulated to restrain each branch from abusing its constitutional authority or usurping power rightfully belonging to the other branches, the states, or the people. At the same time, they promote cooperation between the president and Congress. Some checks and balances have already been noted. The following illustrates how they come into play with legislation.

After passing a bill, Congress sends it to the White House. If the president approves of the measure, he signs it into law. If he disapproves, he can veto the legislation. That sends the bill back to Congress, where it dies or is once again put to a vote. If two-thirds of the legislators in each chamber vote in favor, the veto is overridden and the bill becomes law despite the president's objection.

Once a bill becomes law, the judicial branch can determine the effect of the law by ruling on relevant cases brought before the court. In such lawsuits, a federal court may strike down the law as unconstitutional. This essentially nullifies the law and makes it unenforceable.*

Other checks and balances include the following:

- The president has to rely on Congress for funding.
- International treaties negotiated by the executive branch are not binding without the concurrence of two-thirds of the Senate.
- The president can pardon citizens before or after their federal criminal trials, exempting them from criminal punishment.
- Cabinet secretaries and ambassadors nominated by the president are appointed only if the Senate confirms those nominations.
- Congress can impeach civil officers of the United States, including the president and federal judges, and remove them from office for serious misconduct.†

The ultimate power in a republic, and the greatest check and balance, rests with voters who participate in honest elections to choose fellow citizens to run the government.‡

* *The Constitution does not expressly grant this authority to federal courts. Judicial review is assumed to be an implied power. In 1803 the Supreme Court's landmark ruling in* Marbury v. Madison *marked the first time the judiciary declared a law or part of a law enacted by Congress and the president to be a violation of the Constitution.*

† *Each chamber of Congress may expel one of its own members with a two-thirds vote.*

‡ *Voters have the power every two years to replace 88% of the Congress, i.e., the entire House of Representatives (435 members) and one-third of the Senate (33-34 members).*

21
PRESIDENT WASHINGTON and the BILL OF RIGHTS

After ratifying the Constitution, the states held federal elections. As expected, George Washington was elected as the nation's first president. The new national government convened in 1789 in New York City. Bringing the Constitution to life in working institutions of effective government for a population of four million was a monumental task.* Washington and the other leaders were keenly aware that everything they did would set precedents and give direction to their successors.

Notwithstanding the constraints that were in place, the early leaders were concerned that a federal government as powerful as the one created by the Constitution might infringe upon personal liberties and states' rights. To explicitly guarantee certain fundamental freedoms, rights, and protections, the first Congress passed ten constitutional amendments that were subsequently ratified by the states. They are known collectively as the Bill of Rights.

1st Amendment – Forbids Congress from making laws respecting an establishment of religion or prohibiting the free exercise thereof. It also guarantees free speech, freedom of the press, the right of the people to peaceably assemble, and the right to petition the government for a redress of grievances.

2nd Amendment – Prohibits infringement of the right of the people to keep and bear arms.

3rd Amendment – Forbids the military from forcibly using private homes for lodging.

4th Amendment – Protects against unreasonable searches and seizures.

5th Amendment – Guarantees the right to due process of law. It protects a person from being tried twice for the same crime (double jeopardy) or from being compelled to be a witness against himself (the basis for the right to remain silent in police interrogations).
In addition, the amendment guarantees fair compensation for private property taken for public use, a process known as eminent domain.

6th Amendment – Guarantees a speedy public trial by an impartial jury in criminal prosecutions. The accused also has the right to confront his accuser(s), gather defense witnesses, and have the assistance of an attorney.

7th Amendment – Guarantees the right to a jury trial in certain civil cases.

8th Amendment – Protects against cruel and unusual punishment and excessive fines or bails.

9th and 10th Amendments – Reserves to the states or the people all rights and powers not enumerated by the Constitution and delegated to the federal government.

Amending the Constitution is a two-step process of congressional approval and state ratification; the president is not directly involved. A proposed amendment must first pass by a two-thirds majority in both chambers of Congress (at least 290 in the House and 67 in the Senate).† It is then presented to the state legislatures or to special state conventions for ratification. If three-fourths of the states (at least 38) vote in favor, the amendment is adopted and becomes binding throughout the country. The Constitution has been amended 27 times, most recently in 1992 over the issue of congressional pay raises.

* *According to the latest census, the U.S. population in 2020 was 331 million, a 7% increase over the 309 million counted in 2010.*

† *Article V of the Constitution permits an alternative method for proposing amendments. The legislatures in two-thirds of the states (at least 34) may call a national convention for that purpose, but they have never done so.*

22
POLITICAL PARTIES, WASHINGTON D.C., and LOUISIANA

Political parties are civic organizations whose objective is to gain power in the government. They strive to choose the best candidates from their membership to compete for elective office against candidates from opposing parties. The Constitution makes no mention of political parties, but it was not long before two parties emerged with different visions for the future of the country. The Federalists, led by Alexander Hamilton, believed a strong central government was necessary for America to grow as a commercial power. The Democratic-Republicans viewed the nation as an agricultural republic and resisted efforts to strengthen the federal government at the expense of states' rights. Their leader was Thomas Jefferson.*

In 1790, the seat of the federal government moved from New York to Philadelphia until a permanent capital in a separate jurisdiction from the states could be designated and built. President Washington chose a site along the Potomac River, land that had been part of Maryland and Virginia. It was named Washington, D.C. (District of Columbia).†

By the year 1800, construction on the Capitol building and the White House was far enough along for the government to move to the new capital. George Washington's successor, John Adams of Massachusetts, was the first president to reside in the executive mansion.

The territory claimed by the United States extended only as far west as the Mississippi River. That waterway, with the port of New Orleans near its mouth, was an important channel of commerce for the new republic. Most of the land westward to the Rocky Mountains was known as Louisiana and was largely uncharted. In 1682, the French laid claim to this vast territory (named after their monarch, Louis XIV), but they ceded it to Spain in 1762 during the French and Indian War.

France reacquired Louisiana in 1800 through a secret treaty with Spain. After the deal came to light, Thomas Jefferson, the third U.S. president, sent envoys to France to negotiate the purchase of New Orleans, a vital hub for Americans transferring cargo to and from seagoing vessels. Surprisingly, the French emperor, Napoleon, offered to sell not just the city, but all of Louisiana for only $15 million. The Louisiana Purchase, an acquisition of 530 million acres, nearly doubled the size of the United States in 1803 for less than 3¢ an acre.

President Jefferson was eager to know more about the newly acquired Louisiana Territory and what lay beyond it. He appointed Meriwether Lewis, his secretary who was also an army captain, to organize and lead a military unit known as the Corps of Discovery. Its mission was to map the area, evaluate the land's fertility and mineral deposits, conduct scientific research on plants and wildlife, find the Northwest Passage to the Pacific Ocean, and establish peaceful relations with the Native Americans and learn about their cultures. Lewis chose William Clark, his former commanding officer, to help lead the venture.

In 1804 the Corps of Discovery left St. Louis and headed up the Missouri River, the nation's longest river. In present-day North Dakota, a French-Canadian fur trapper, his Indian wife, Sacagawea, and their infant son joined the exploratory expedition. Tribes encountered on the trip regarded the presence of a woman and her child as an indication that the 33-member party, made up mostly of soldiers, was not a threat. Her knowledge of edible wild plants proved valuable when provisions ran low. To cross the Rockies, the group obtained horses from a Shoshone chief who was Sacagawea's relative.

Lewis and Clark's epic journey, all the way to the Pacific Northwest coast and back, lasted 28 months and covered 8,000 miles. They did not find a Northwest Passage, but the specimens they brought back in 1806 and their maps and detailed journals provided ample evidence of the mission's success. It sparked the imagination of Americans and gave them a sense of the adventure to be found in the West.

* *Various political parties have come and gone since the nation's founding. For more than 150 years, there have been two main political parties in the United States: the Democratic Party, symbolized by a donkey, and the Republican Party (also known as the Grand Old Party, or GOP), symbolized by an elephant.*

† *The capital city, named for George Washington, was originally only part of a much larger federal district named Columbia, derived from Columbus. Columbia is a female figure first used in colonial times to symbolize the American continent. Later she came to also represent, more specifically, the United States. Her image has appeared on U.S. coins and stamps.*

Lewis & Clark, Sacagawea, her husband, and Clark's slave

White House set ablaze by British troops

Erie Canal

Francis Scott Key at the Battle of Fort McHenry

Water-powered mill

Early steam locomotive

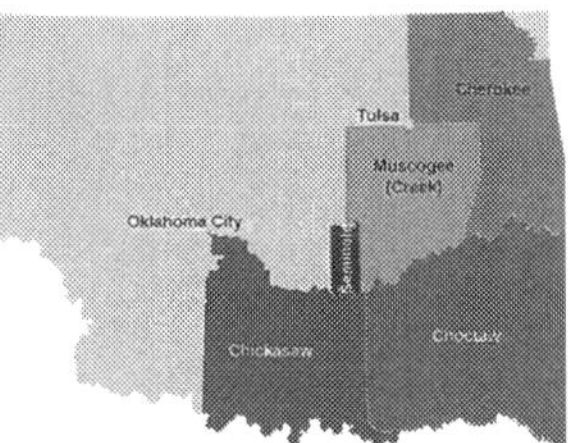

Tribal boundaries in Oklahoma after the Trail of Tears

Slave ship

President Andrew Jackson

Running cotton through a gin

Slave family picking cotton

Harriet Tubman

Frederick Douglass

The Alamo

U.S. troops enter Mexico City

Sutter's Mill

Miner pans for gold

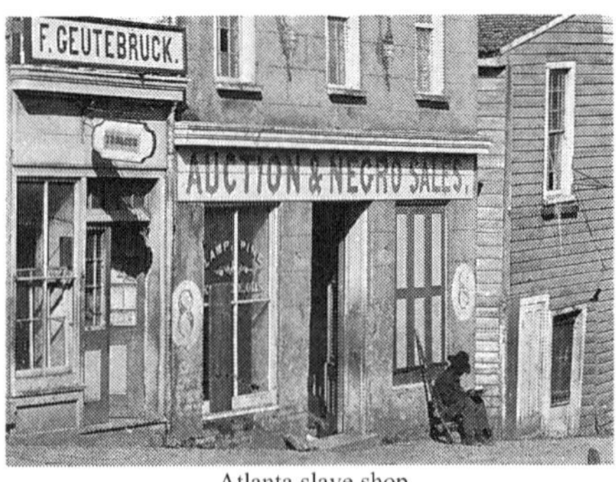

Atlanta slave shop

Spirit of the Frontier

Pioneers heading westward

Oregon Territory

President James K. Polk

23
THE DAWN'S EARLY LIGHT and BARBARY PIRATES

Relations between the United States and Great Britain, tenuous following the Revolution, deteriorated after 1805 and pushed the countries toward war again, which held out the possibility of the U.S. acquiring territory in Canada and Florida.

American settlers along the northern U.S. border accused the British of supplying arms to Native Americans and inciting them to attack. At sea, hostile actions by the British navy were harming America's maritime trade. Already at war with France, the British blockaded continental Europe and seized American merchant ships that ignored the restriction. Britain also stepped up its policy of impressment, forcing sailors abducted from American ships to serve in the Royal Navy. Some of the sailors were British deserters, but others were U.S. citizens by birth or through naturalization, which the British did not acknowledge. They regarded men born in England as English subjects for life and, therefore, obligated to serve in their military. "Once an Englishman, always an Englishman."

After declaring war on Britain in 1812, the U.S. suffered a number of setbacks in the Great Lakes region before 28-year-old Commodore Oliver H. Perry's heroic actions forced an entire British naval squadron to surrender at the Battle of Lake Erie. The low point of the war came in 1814 when redcoats marched into Washington, D.C., and set fire to the White House, the Capitol, the Library of Congress, and other buildings. A violent storm and a rare tornado did further damage but also put out the fires and hastened the departure of the enemy troops.

British forces sailed up the Chesapeake Bay intent on taking the city of Baltimore. Fort McHenry, situated at the entrance to Baltimore Harbor, stood in their way. As the British bombarded the fort through the night, an American lawyer, Francis Scott Key, watched from a nearby ship. James Madison, the nation's fourth president, had given him permission to negotiate the release of a U.S. citizen being held on an English vessel. He secured the man's freedom, but British naval commanders detained both men until after the battle. Early the next day, Key saw the U.S. flag still flying over Fort McHenry. Inspired by the successful defense of the fort, he wrote a poem to be sung to a popular tune of the day. "The Star-Spangled Banner" became a revered patriotic song in America.* The first of four stanzas reads:

> Oh say, can you see, by the dawn's early light,
> What so proudly we hailed at the twilight's last gleaming?
> Whose broad stripes and bright stars, through the perilous fight,

O'er the ramparts† we watched, were so gallantly streaming?
And the rockets' red glare, the bombs bursting in air,
Gave proof through the night that our flag was still there.
Oh say, does that Star-Spangled Banner yet wave
O'er the land of the free and the home of the brave?

Just days before the Battle of Fort McHenry, U.S. naval forces in upstate New York led by Commandant Thomas Macdonough masterfully repulsed a large British invasion out of Canada at the Battle of Lake Champlain (also known as the Battle of Plattsburgh).

Negotiations to end the conflict were already underway in Belgium. The Treaty of Ghent, signed by diplomats on Christmas Eve in 1814, called for an end to hostilities and a restoration of pre-war boundaries without addressing the principal issues that led to the taking up of arms. The government in London accepted the treaty before the end of the year, but the war continued until both nations approved the document.

New Orleans was the site of a major battle in late December and early January. U.S. General Andrew Jackson, leading a diverse force of army regulars, state militias, slaves, free blacks, Creoles, Choctaw Indians, and Jean Lafitte's band of pirates, fortified a line of defense against the more numerous enemy. The British lost 2,400 troops before retreating. American forces suffered 300 casualties.

The U.S. Senate ratified the Treaty of Ghent in February of 1815, bringing the war to a close. The War of 1812, sometimes called the second war of independence, created a strong feeling of national unity and pride even though it ended in a draw. America showed that it was willing and able to stand alone and defend itself against the most powerful nation in the world.

Shortly after that war ended, the United States asserted its military strength across the Atlantic. For centuries, North Africa's Barbary states – Algeria, Tunisia, Tripoli (Libya), and Morocco – had supported pirates who terrorized the Mediterranean: raiding coastal towns, seizing foreign ships, and plundering their cargoes. Those taken hostage were held for ransom or sold into slavery. The Barbary rulers exacted tribute from European nations (and later the U.S.) in return for unmolested transit.

By the time the First Barbary War began in 1801, the United States had already paid $2 million. In 1805 a U.S. force consisting of eight Marines and hundreds of mostly Arab mercenaries marched 500 miles across the desert "to the shores of Tripoli." With U.S. naval support, they captured the port city of Derna and rescued 300 American sailors being held hostage. The war ended shortly thereafter.

But the piracy did not stop permanently, and the United States intervened again. In 1815, a fleet of 10 warships under the command of

Stephen Decatur entered the Mediterranean Sea. The Navy forced the Barbary states to return American prisoners and property, pay restitution, and cease attacks on American shipping once and for all. The U.S. ended its tribute payments, and European nations followed suit.

* *"The Star-Spangled Banner" did not become the national anthem until 1931, more than a hundred years after the Battle of Fort McHenry.*

† *walls of the fort*

24
WESTWARD MIGRATION and INDUSTRIALIZATION

From the time of their first settlements on the East Coast, Americans kept pushing westward. For those who went, the adventure of settling new territory and the prospect of acquiring land for free or at a low cost outweighed the hardships and dangers of frontier life.

Western migration increased after the War of 1812. The construction of roads and canals made it easier for people to travel and transport goods. The Cumberland Road, also called the National Road, was one of the first major improved highways in the country. It provided a land route between two important rivers, the Potomac and the Ohio, and continued westward into Illinois.*

The most significant man-made waterway was the Erie Canal, which stretched for 360 miles across New York State, from the Hudson River in the east to Lake Erie in the west. Initially four feet deep and 40 feet wide, the canal opened up another water route between the Great Lakes and the Atlantic Ocean. Horses, mules, or oxen hitched up to long ropes towed boats and barges up and down the canal.

Northern states experienced a rapid growth in industrialization: the use of machines to manufacture goods in larger quantities and often of higher quality than is possible with human labor alone. The first manufacturing plants, built along rivers, used the flowing water to power the machinery. With the advent of steam-powered engines, mechanized plants could operate virtually anywhere. Steam engines also propelled boats and trains at speeds that drastically reduced transportation times.

The South lagged far behind the North in the Industrial Revolution. Agriculture, the largest economic sector in both regions, was more dominant in the South, which enjoyed a longer growing season and had more large farms, or plantations.

* *The Great Wagon Road, built in colonial times, ran through the Appalachian Valley from Pennsylvania to Tennessee with a branch running farther south to Georgia.*

25
SLAVERY

Slavery was an integral part of Southern life.* Its roots in the U.S. went back to colonial times, possibly to Jamestown. It was there in 1619 that a Dutch ship arrived with 20 African captives on board.† John Rolfe paid for them, but it is unclear if their status in Virginia was that of slaves or indentured servants. The latter were obligated to work for a set period of time (typically four to seven years) in exchange for the voyage to America, room and board, or other compensation that might include a parcel of land. Such arrangements were usually voluntary, and the servant had legal rights. During the colonial era and after the Revolutionary War, many Europeans came to America as indentured servants, but for Africans – involuntary, permanent, and inheritable servitude was the norm. Slaves were considered property.

The slaves came from African cultures with long-distance trade networks and diverse social and political systems. Many different languages were spoken on the continent. Africans created complex musical forms and works of art, and they were skilled metalworkers. Gold was a major export. For centuries before Europeans entered the slave market, Africans had been enslaved and traded by other Africans and Arabs.

The plantation system in many European colonies in the Americas created a huge demand for labor, and Africa became the main supplier.‡ Men, women, and children on the continent were abducted by other Africans and marched to the coast, where they became inventory for African slave merchants to trade with their European counterparts. A slave might be thrown in with captives taken from different parts of Africa whose language and culture were foreign. Some slaves were branded with a hot iron to identify them as the property of a specific owner.

The first major European slave merchants were from Spain, Portugal, and the Netherlands. By the 18th century, England had become the foremost slave-trading nation.

Most slaves were brought to the Western Hemisphere in an economic cycle known as the Transatlantic Triangular Trade. European merchants sailed to Africa with guns, textiles, rum, and other manufactured goods to barter for gold, ivory, and slaves. The captives, often stripped of clothing, were packed onto the ships like cargo for the next leg of the journey, the notorious Middle Passage across the Atlantic. The horrendous conditions drove some slaves to commit suicide by jumping into the sea. In a few known cases, slaves who fell ill were thrown overboard to keep them from infecting other slaves and because the ship's insurance covered deaths due to drowning but not disease. Those who survived the crossing were traded for New World goods, which were loaded onto the ships for the return voyage to Europe to complete the triangle.[§]

Twelve and a half million Africans, a fifth of them children, were taken from their homelands for transport to the Western Hemisphere. Around two million died en route. The vast majority of slaves went to European colonies in South America and the Caribbean. The Portuguese colony of Brazil imported the most slaves by far, close to five million, or 46 percent of the total. The number of slaves brought from Africa to the Thirteen Colonies (and later the U.S.) was small by comparison: 390,000, or four percent of the total brought to the Americas.[¶]

Several of the nation's Founders, including George Washington, Thomas Jefferson, and James Madison, all Southern planters from Virginia, owned slaves. The Constitution addressed slavery in three clauses. The first dealt with taxation and representation. Southern delegates to the Constitutional Convention wanted to include slaves in the population count used to determine representation in Congress but exclude them for tax purposes. The convention compromised by including 60 percent (3/5) of a state's slave population in the basis for both representation and direct taxes.

The second slavery clause in the Constitution prohibited any restriction on the importation of slaves before the year 1808. The third clause stipulated that slaves could not win their freedom by escaping across state lines and had to be returned to their masters if apprehended.

In 1793 Eli Whitney invented a machine that removed the seeds from raw cotton fiber. His cotton gin greatly increased the amount of product that could be processed in a day and made the plant a highly lucrative cash crop. Cotton became "king" in the South, and the demand for more slaves grew.[#]

The United States banned the importation of slaves on January 1, 1808, the first day such legislation was permitted by the Constitution,[▲] but the status of slaves already in the country did not change. The slave population more than tripled in the South over the next 50 years due to smuggling and high birth rates.[◊]

Opposition to slavery on moral and religious grounds had existed from colonial times. That opposition dwindled in the South but grew more determined in the North.

* *At the dawn of the 19th century, the slave population was 21,000 in New York and 12,000 in New Jersey, but overall, slavery was not practiced on a large scale in the North, although far more slave voyages originated there, especially in Rhode Island. Northern slave voyages typically deposited their African captives in the Caribbean.*

† *The first African slaves in the Western Hemisphere were brought to the Caribbean by Spaniards more than a century earlier, in the early 1500s. By 1619 slavery was*

already well established on plantations throughout Spanish America and in the Portuguese colony of Brazil, where labor-intensive cane sugar was the main export. (The sugarcane plant is native to the Eastern Hemisphere.)
Slavery was common in America before Europeans arrived. After African slavery was introduced, some Native Americans in the Southeast purchased blacks as slaves.

‡ *For the first three centuries after Columbus, the number of Africans brought to the New World far exceeded the number of Europeans who came, by a ratio of six to one. It was the largest forced migration in history.*

§ *There were variations to the triangle. For example, New England merchants shipped rum, fish, and agricultural goods to Africa to trade for slaves, who were transported to the West Indies and exchanged for sugar, molasses, and coffee bound for New England. Thousands of slaves originally brought to the West Indies were subsequently transported to the Thirteen Colonies (and later the United States).*

¶ *Distribution of the roughly 10½ million African slaves brought to the New World:*

4.9 million	*46%*	*Portuguese Brazil*	*440,000*	*4%*	*Dutch Americas*
2.3 million	*22%*	*British Caribbean*	*390,000*	*4%*	*Thirteen Colonies/U.S.*
1.3 million	*12%*	*Spanish Americas*	*110,000*	*1%*	*Danish Caribbean*
1.1 million	*11%*	*French Caribbean*			

Most slaves worked in agriculture, but others were skilled laborers such as coopers, blacksmiths, carpenters, and cooks. Slaves were sometimes hired out to supplement their owners' income.

▲ *The bill banning the importation of slaves was signed into law by President Thomas Jefferson.*

◊ *The Southern slave population in 1810 was 1.2 million. By 1860 it had risen to four million. In South Carolina and Mississippi, slaves outnumbered the rest of the population.*

26
MISSOURI COMPROMISE and the MONROE DOCTRINE

Population growth in the U.S. territories west of the first 13 states led to the creation of new states. By 1819, there were 22 states in the country. The 11 "free" states in the North either prohibited slavery or were in the process of abolishing it. They were:

Massachusetts	New Hampshire	New Jersey	Indiana
Rhode Island	Vermont	Pennsylvania	Illinois
Connecticut	New York	Ohio	

Slavery was legal in the 11 Southern states:

Virginia	North Carolina	Kentucky	Mississippi
Maryland	South Carolina	Tennessee	Alabama
Delaware	Georgia	Louisiana	

With the same number of Northern free states and Southern slave states, each side was equally represented in the U.S. Senate.

A conflict arose when Missouri applied for statehood. Slavery was already established in the territory. Allowing Missouri to become a state would tip the balance in the Senate in favor of slave states. In 1820, Congress reached an agreement known as the Missouri Compromise. Maine, which was part of Massachusetts, would be admitted as a free state to balance Missouri's admission as a slave state. The legislation banned slavery in the rest of the Louisiana Territory north of the latitude line corresponding to Missouri's southern border.*

The Missouri Compromise did not end the debate. Continued Northern opposition to slavery threatened the South's economy and social order. John Adams and Thomas Jefferson worried that the brewing tensions might erupt into a civil war and split the nation they helped found.†

In foreign affairs, an independence movement was underway in Latin America. Colombia separated from Spain in 1810. Over the next 12 years, Mexico and most of the other Spanish colonies also declared independence. In 1822 Brazil broke away from Portugal. To the north, Russia laid claim to territory in the Pacific Northwest. These developments raised concerns that European nations might try to regain or increase their influence in the Americas. It was in this context in 1823 that President James Monroe made a bold declaration of U.S. foreign policy. The Monroe Doctrine asserted that:

- European nations should not consider North or South America for any future colonization.
- Any attempt by a European power to extend its political system to any part of the Western Hemisphere would be regarded as dangerous to the peace and safety of the United States.
- The U.S. would not meddle in the internal affairs of European nations or interfere with their existing colonies in the Americas.

* *The Missouri Compromise Line should not be confused with the Mason-Dixon Line, established in colonial times to settle a border dispute between Pennsylvania and Maryland. The Mason-Dixon Line came to symbolize the cultural boundary between the North and the South.*

† *Both men died on the Fourth of July in 1826, Jefferson at age 83 and Adams at 90.*

27
JACKSONIAN DEMOCRACY and TARIFFS

The Constitution left it up to the states to determine who was eligible to vote in elections. Early on, one had to be a taxpayer or own a certain amount of property. In some states, being a Catholic, Jew, or Quaker was disqualifying. The gradual lifting of those restrictions led to a widening of political participation in the country and paved the way for Andrew Jackson's presidency (1829-37).

Born in humble circumstances in the backwoods of the Carolinas without the advantages of earlier presidents, Jackson had a natural appeal to the common man. He fought in the Revolutionary War as a boy, moved to Tennessee in his early twenties to practice law, represented the state in both chambers of the U.S. Congress, and served as a judge on the state Superior Court before becoming a hero in the War of 1812. He also led troops against Native Americans and Spaniards and served as the first territorial governor of Florida.

In 1828 he was elected from Tennessee as the seventh president of the United States and was the first from an interior state. His political philosophy, which became known as "Jacksonian democracy," included fiscal discipline,* more assertive presidential leadership, opposition to banks (especially the national bank), selling public land to settlers at low prices, and rewarding loyal supporters with government positions (political patronage, or the "spoils system").

President Jackson had to confront the growing sectionalism in the country. Slavery was not the only issue dividing the North and the South; sharp disagreements arose over tariffs as well.

A tariff is a tax on imported goods. Besides being a source of revenue for the federal government,† tariffs (also called duties) are a means of protecting domestic producers from foreign competition.

To illustrate how tariffs work, assume that American stores sell only two kinds of chairs, those imported from France that sell for $10 apiece and those made in America that sell for $12. Most consumers would buy the cheaper French chair. With more of their chairs being sold, French chair manufacturers make more money, build more factories, and hire more French workers.

If the federal government adds a $5 tariff to French chairs, most U.S. consumers would buy the now-cheaper American chairs.‡ With more of their product being sold, American chair manufacturers make more money, build more factories, and hire more American workers. Some people would continue to buy French chairs, however, even at the higher price, if they had a strong preference for the foreign product or if domestic manufacturers could not produce a sufficient quantity of chairs to satisfy consumer demand. The tariffs, collected from American importers, flow into the U.S. treasury.

French Chair		American Chair
$10	price before tariff	$12
+ 5	U.S. tariff on French chairs	n/a
$15	price after tariff	$12

The government can levy tariffs on raw materials and farm products as well as manufactured goods.

U.S. imports fell sharply during the Napoleonic Wars in Europe and the War of 1812. The difficulty of procuring manufactured goods from abroad highlighted the need for an American industrial base as a matter of national security and to broaden an economy dominated by agriculture and shipping. Manufacturing was growing in the Northern states, but European industry was more established, especially in Britain, and could produce goods more efficiently and cheaply, even with the added cost of transatlantic shipping to America factored in.

The United States raised tariffs in 1816, 1824, and 1828 to protect domestic manufacturers from lower-priced imports and help infant American industries develop a home market. The rates of the 1828 tariff were so exorbitant that Southerners called it the "Tariff of Abominations."

When the federal government laid a tariff on a product, all U.S. consumers who were accustomed to buying cheaper imports of that product had to pay more – those who switched to buying American and those who continued buying the foreign product, now laden with a tariff. The higher prices were more palatable to Northerners because of the benefits tariffs brought to their region. Tariffs resulted in increased sales for Northern manufacturers and more jobs for Northern workers. Since most of their production was for the domestic market, Northerners did not have to worry about the effect American tariffs had overseas.

For Southerners, there was no silver lining to the higher prices they had to pay for products affected by the tariffs. The region had relatively few manufacturing businesses and workers that could benefit from such governmental protection. Moreover, Southerners relied heavily on sales of their agricultural products abroad. Cotton alone accounted for over half of all U.S. exports. Retaliatory tariffs by foreign countries could close off those lucrative markets.

Southerners viewed the tariffs as a backdoor attempt to abolish slavery and questioned their constitutionality because they showed preference to certain states.

The U.S. lowered tariff rates in 1832 but not enough to placate South Carolina. The state legislature called for a special state convention to consider the matter. Delegates to the convention passed an ordinance that nullified the tariffs of 1828 and 1832, declared them unconstitutional, forbade the collection of duties in the state, and threatened secession from the United States if the federal government tried to force their compliance. By assuming a right to secede and a right to unilaterally repeal federal law, South Carolina challenged the supremacy of the national government and the Constitution.

To show that he fully intended to enforce the nation's tariff laws, President Jackson, though a Southerner and a slaveholder, sent naval ships and a contingent of soldiers to reinforce two forts in Charleston Harbor. A violent confrontation between federal troops and the state militia was averted when the U.S. Congress passed a bill in 1833 that reduced tariffs even further, and South Carolina rescinded its nullification ordinance.

* *Jackson is the only president in U.S. history to pay off the national debt.*

† *From 1789 to 1909, tariffs were the largest source of federal revenue in all but 12 years.*

‡ *Manufacturers, wholesalers, and retailers can mitigate a tariff's effect on price by accepting lower profit margins.*

28
TRAIL of TEARS, MANIFEST DESTINY, and GOLD

Congress passed the Indian Removal Act in 1830 authorizing President Jackson to grant federal territory west of the Mississippi River to tribes who relinquished their ancestral lands. The government promised to assist with the relocation and protect the Indians after they arrived at their assigned destinations, most of which were in present-day Oklahoma. The exodus of Native Americans (especially the Cherokee) from the Southern states is remembered as the "Trail of Tears" because of the cruelty and privation they experienced.

In the 1820s, the newly independent nation of Mexico allowed an American, Stephen Austin, to bring settlers into its territory in present-day Texas to help Mexican residents ward off Indian attacks, but the huge influx that followed alarmed Mexican officials. When Mexico tried to reassert control over the region, the settlers fought back.

The most famous battle took place in 1836 at the Alamo, a San Antonio fort that was originally a Spanish mission. Two hundred men, American settlers and volunteers from the United States, were determined to hold the fort. The garrison included American folk heroes Davy Crockett and Jim Bowie. A Mexican army of 3,000 led by General Santa Anna laid siege to the Alamo for 13 days before finally overwhelming and killing the defenders.

The remaining Texas forces, led by Sam Houston, rallied and defeated Santa Anna the next month. Texans had already declared independence and formed a new nation: the Republic of Texas. In 1845 Texas joined the U.S. as the 28th state.

The United States declared war on Mexico in 1846 after Mexicans attacked American troops in a disputed area along the Rio Grande (Big River). The following year, the U.S. military captured the enemy's capital, Mexico City, and occupied the National Palace, or "the halls of Montezuma." *

In the Treaty of Guadalupe Hidalgo that ended the Mexican War in 1848, Mexico ceded 40 percent of its territory, which included present-day California, Nevada, Utah, most of Arizona, and parts of New Mexico, Colorado, and Wyoming. The United States agreed to pay Mexico $15 million and satisfy up to $3.25 million in claims filed by Americans against the Mexican government. The 75,000 Mexicans living in what was now U.S. territory would become American citizens by default after one year if they did not exercise their option to retain Mexican citizenship. Most became U.S. citizens.

Before the war ended, members of The Church of Jesus Christ of Latter-day Saints, commonly known as Mormons, entered the desolate Salt Lake Valley in the Great Basin. They had crossed the Plains and the Rocky Mountains after mobs in Illinois killed their prophet and church founder, Joseph Smith, and drove them from the state. Under the leadership of Smith's successor, Brigham Young, members of the church established hundreds of settlements in Utah and other parts of the West.

In the Northwest, the United States and Great Britain resolved a disagreement over the Oregon Territory without war. A treaty in 1846 made the present-day states of Oregon, Washington, Idaho, and parts of Montana and Wyoming undisputed U.S. territory.

The Oregon Territory, the Mexican Cession, and Texas all became part of the United States during James K. Polk's presidency (1845-49). This additional 600 million acres, more land than was acquired with the Louisiana Purchase, extended the country's western boundary to the Pacific Ocean.† Americans believed the expansion across the continent was "Manifest Destiny," or obvious and inevitable.

In 1848 gold was discovered near Sacramento, California, at a sawmill belonging to John Sutter. The news spread quickly and spawned a gold rush. Eighty thousand "49ers" streamed into California the next year. Discoveries of gold and silver in Nevada, Colorado, and elsewhere also drew thousands of prospectors westward.

During this same period, European and Asian immigrants came to America in large numbers to seek greater economic opportunity and escape political unrest. A million immigrants came from Ireland alone due to a potato famine there.

* *Montezuma, king of the Aztecs, reigned over central Mexico before conquistador Hernando Cortés conquered that indigenous culture in 1521 with a small Spanish force.*

† *Nineteen million additional acres acquired from Mexico in 1854 extended the southern borders of Arizona and New Mexico. The Gadsden Purchase is named for U.S. diplomat James Gadsden, who negotiated the $10 million deal.*

29
ABOLITION

Abolitionists wanted to end slavery throughout the U.S., and some were willing to violate fugitive slave laws. They organized the Underground Railroad, a network of people who hid escaped slaves and secretly transported them to free states and Canada instead of returning them to their masters, as required by law. Harriet Tubman is called "the Moses of her people" for leading hundreds to freedom after she escaped from her slave master.*

The most prominent abolitionist was Frederick Douglass, also an escaped slave. The success of his autobiography in America and Europe and his eloquent and moving speeches helped dispel the notion that blacks were inherently intellectually inferior. While he was lecturing in England, his friends paid off his former master, making Douglass legally free.†

In 1852 Harriet Beecher Stowe published her novel, *Uncle Tom's Cabin*. Inspired by fugitive slave laws, it portrayed the evils of slavery in a dramatic manner and had a significant impact on public opinion in the North.

The Kansas-Nebraska Act, signed by President Franklin Pierce in 1854, carved two new territories out of part of the Louisiana Territory. In a concession to pro-slavery factions, a "popular sovereignty" provision in the legislation left it up to the electorate in each territory to decide whether to allow slavery. Both territories were north of Missouri's southern border and supposedly already off limits to slavery, according to the Missouri Compromise of 1820. This angered Northerners and led to the formation of a new political party: the Republican Party.

Nebraska was too far north to attract slaveholders, but Kansas became a battleground. Supporters and opponents of slavery came into the territory hoping to sway the vote. Deadly clashes between the two groups left more than 50 people dead and earned the territory the nickname "Bleeding Kansas" before it was admitted to the U.S. as a free state.

The Supreme Court handed down a ruling in 1857 known as the Dred Scott decision. Dred Scott, a slave owned by a Missouri surgeon, had lived for a time with his master in the Wisconsin Territory and in the state of Illinois. Scott filed suit on the grounds that residing even temporarily where slavery was illegal had made him a free man. The high court disagreed. A majority of the justices held that slaves were property with no constitutional rights, and the Missouri Compromise's ban on slavery in the upper Louisiana Territory was unconstitutional. Southerners hailed the decision. Northerners were outraged.

John Brown, a radical abolitionist, believed he was an instrument of God to help end slavery. In 1859 he and several accomplices failed in their attempt to seize the federal arsenal at Harpers Ferry, in western Virginia. They had planned to lead slaves in an armed uprising. Authorities hanged Brown and six others after they were convicted of murder, treason, and conspiring to produce an insurrection. Northern abolitionists regarded him as a martyr. In the South, Harpers Ferry stoked longstanding fears of a widespread slave revolt.‡

* *On 13 personal missions before the Civil War, Tubman rescued 70 slaves in Maryland. During the war, she helped Union troops free 756 slaves in a raid on the Combahee River in South Carolina.*

† *Besides the four million slaves, there were 500,000 free African-Americans in the U.S. in 1860, with slightly more in the South than in the North. Some had emigrated from foreign lands as free people. Many blacks in Louisiana had been free under French and Spanish rule, and they maintained that status after the Louisiana Purchase.*

As for former slaves, some had gained their freedom by serving in the military or through state manumission laws in the North. Others were freed as a result of interracial intimacy or were simply let go when they became sick or old or when their masters died. Thousands of free blacks in the South were slaveholders.

‡ *In 1831 Nat Turner, a 30-year-old slave on a Virginia plantation, led a band of fellow slaves and a few free blacks in an attack on whites. Over the course of two days, they slaughtered 55 people, mostly women and children. Whites trying to quell the revolt and seeking revenge killed an even greater number of innocent blacks. Local authorities hanged Turner and 17 of his followers after trying them in court.*

30
ABRAHAM LINCOLN, SECESSION, and CIVIL WAR

Tensions between the North and South reached a critical stage in 1860 when the Republican Party's candidate, Abraham Lincoln of Illinois, was elected the 16th U.S. president. Lincoln opposed slavery, but he felt that the nation breaking apart over the issue was worse. His compromise was to let slavery continue where it already existed while prohibiting its expansion into the western territories. That position was unacceptable in a large part of the South even though only a quarter of the households owned slaves. Southerners, most of whom were Democrats, believed slavery was essential to their economy and way of life. Limiting its expansion was considered a threat to the region.

Before Lincoln took office, Southern states began breaking away from the United States. South Carolina was first. Mississippi, Florida,* Alabama, Georgia, Louisiana, and Texas soon followed. They formed a separate nation known as the Confederate States of America and chose Jefferson Davis of Mississippi as their president.†

President Lincoln pleaded for reconciliation in his inaugural address.

> We are not enemies, but friends. We must not be enemies. Though passion may have strained, it must not break our bonds of affection. The mystic chords of memory, stretching from every battlefield and patriot grave to every living heart and hearthstone all over this broad land, will yet swell the chorus of the Union, when again touched, as surely they will be, by the better angels of our nature.

Southerners were unmoved. States that seceded took possession of federal property within their borders. Fort Sumter, however, situated on a small man-made island at the entrance to the harbor in Charleston, South Carolina, remained in federal hands. By April 1861, provisions at the fort were running low. President Lincoln notified South Carolina that he was sending ships to resupply the fort. On the morning of April 12, before the ships arrived, rebels began bombarding the fort, igniting a civil war in America. The garrison of 80 federal troops surrendered the next day.

After the fall of Fort Sumter, four more Southern states seceded: Virginia, Arkansas, Tennessee, and North Carolina. The Confederacy established its capital in Richmond, Virginia – just 100 miles south of Washington, D.C.

Missouri, Kentucky, Maryland, and Delaware – the Southern slave states bordering the free states of the North – did not join the Confederacy. Also, the northwestern counties of Virginia refused to follow the decision of their state legislature to secede. That region became a new state: West Virginia.[‡] Although these border states remained in the Union, they were, nevertheless, home to many Confederate sympathizers and contributed soldiers to both armies.

The two sides in the Civil War[§] were differentiated as follows:

Section of the Country	North	South (Dixie)
Government	United States of America / USA / Union	Confederate States of America / CSA / Confederacy
President	Abraham Lincoln	Jefferson Davis
Soldier/Citizen	Yankee	Rebel
Color of Uniform	Blue	Gray

From the outset, the Union had tremendous advantages. Its population in 23 states and the federal territories exceeded 22 million. The population in the 11 Confederate states was less than nine million, 3½ million (40 percent) of whom were slaves. The North had an established army and navy, better roads, more steamboats, barges, and railroads, and more factories to produce weapons and other military supplies.

Furthermore, the political philosophy of the Confederate states worked against them. Their belief in the primacy of states' rights made them averse to the centralization needed to win and limited the Richmond government's ability to finance the war through taxation.

But the South was not without advantages. In the beginning, the Confederacy had more aggressive military leaders and a better cavalry. To win, it had only to maintain defensive positions on familiar terrain. For the North to win, it would have to take the offensive, invade the South, and force Confederate states back into the Union, which would require more resources and longer supply lines. Despite the fact that Europe, with some exceptions, had already abolished slavery, Southerners expected European nations, consumers of their agricultural goods, to come to their aid and pressure the Union to accept the CSA as a legitimate government. The antebellum South produced two-thirds of the world's raw cotton and 80 percent of the cotton used by Britain's textile industry. All of these factors gave Southerners confidence they could win their independence.

* *Spain ceded Florida to the British in 1763 after the French and Indian War but reacquired the territory after the Revolutionary War. In the Adams-Onís Treaty with the United States, Spain lost Florida for good in 1819. As part of the deal, the U.S. agreed to pay up to $5 million in legal claims filed by American citizens against Spain. In 1845 the U.S. admitted Florida as the 27th state.*

† *Jefferson Davis had represented Mississippi in both chambers of the U.S. Congress and was secretary of war in President Franklin Pierce's cabinet. In the latter capacity, he strengthened the military that the Confederacy would eventually have to fight.*

‡ *In 1863, with the Civil War still raging and after the Emancipation Proclamation had been issued, West Virginia was admitted to the United States as a slave state.*

§ *The conflict is sometimes called other names, such as the "War Between the States," because the Confederacy sought secession, not the overthrow of the U.S. government.*

31
ULYSSES S. GRANT, ROBERT E. LEE, and EMANCIPATION

One week after the Civil War began, President Lincoln ordered a naval blockade of Confederate ports. Enforcing a barrier across 3,000 miles of Southern coastline was impossible at first; blockade runners were able to easily slip past the U.S. Navy. But as more and more coastal territory came under Union control over the course of the war, the blockade would help strangle the Confederacy by choking off its imports and exports.*

The first major contest between the Blue and the Gray took place in Virginia at the Battle of Manassas (also known as the Battle of Bull Run), only 30 miles southwest of Washington, D.C. It was fought in 1861, a few months after the fall of Fort Sumter. Each side began the battle with about 30,000 men. Hundreds of citizens came out from Washington to be close to the scene. The outcome was shocking. Before the day was over, spectators and defeated Union soldiers were fleeing back to the safety of the U.S. capital.

The first key battles of 1862 were in Tennessee. Union General Ulysses S. Grant captured 12,000 Rebel soldiers when he took Fort Donelson. Two months later a Confederate attack caught him unprepared at the Battle of Shiloh, but he received reinforcements and rallied his troops to beat back the Rebels, though at a great cost.

The Confederacy suffered a calamity when a Union naval squadron under the command of David Farragut captured New Orleans and closed off the mouth of the Mississippi River, one of the South's main supply routes. The Rebels deployed a new kind of weapon, the ironclad, in their unsuccessful defense of the city. These warships, developed by both Confederate and Union navies, were covered with thick metal plates to deflect bullets and cannon projectiles.

By the middle of 1862, the Union controlled western Tennessee and much of the lower Mississippi River.

It was a different story in the East. After fending off a Union army of 105,000 trying to take Richmond, the Rebels went on the offensive, winning a second battle at Bull Run and capturing the federal arsenal at Harpers Ferry along with 12,500 Union troops. Confederate General Robert E. Lee then led his army 15 miles farther north, across the Potomac River and into western Maryland. At the Battle of Antietam (also known as the Battle of Sharpsburg), Lee almost won, although outnumbered two to one and despite having had his battle plans carelessly fall into Union hands. The combined 3,600 dead and 17,000 wounded made Antietam the bloodiest single day of the war. Later that year, the Confederacy scored a victory at Fredericksburg, Virginia.

On January 1, 1863, President Lincoln, acting under his war powers as commander-in-chief, issued an executive order[†] known as the Emancipation Proclamation. It made slaves "forever free" but only legally, and the directive applied only to those slaves living in areas of the South still controlled by the Rebels. It would take the Union military to make their freedom a physical reality. Ironically, the order did not abolish slavery in parts of the Confederacy already defeated by Union soldiers, nor did it grant freedom to slaves in the border states that had stayed in the Union. Declaring universal emancipation might have driven those border slave states to secede.

Nevertheless, the proclamation marked the first time Lincoln formally made the abolition of slavery a principal aim of the war.‡ It struck at the heart of the Confederacy's ability to wage war and dashed Southern hopes of receiving diplomatic recognition from Europe. The large number of slaves escaping to Union army lines had helped bring about the change in policy.

The Emancipation Proclamation also authorized the enlistment of freed slaves for military service. Around 180,000 blacks served in the U.S. Army during the war, and another 19,000 joined the Navy.

* *Confederate states voluntarily halted cotton exports in 1861 to force Europe to support the South, but the move failed diplomatically and ravaged the Southern economy.*

† *Article II of the Constitution and certain federal statutes give the president broad authority to issue executive orders to manage the federal government. Like legislation and regulations, executive orders may be challenged in federal court.*

‡ *Preserving the Union had been the principal aim of the war. Lincoln lost considerable public support by elevating abolition to that same status. A drop in the number of volunteers joining the Army compelled Congress to institute a national draft, the first in U.S. history, which sparked riots in New York City.*

32
GETTYSBURG

In Virginia in May of 1863, a Confederate army led by Robert E. Lee defeated a much larger Union army at Chancellorsville. During the battle, Lee's reliable officer, Thomas "Stonewall" Jackson, was returning to the Confederate lines at night when he was shot by a North Carolina regiment that mistook him and his staff for Yankees. Thought to be recovering after the amputation of his left arm, he contracted pneumonia and died eight days after being shot. He had earned his nickname by being fearless and unyielding in battle.

Jackson's death was a blow to General Lee and the Confederacy, but, encouraged by the victory at Chancellorsville, Lee led his troops into the North. He hoped to inflict such heavy losses on the Union army that President Lincoln would be pressured to sue for peace.

The two armies clashed at the small Pennsylvania town of Gettysburg. Seventy-five thousand Rebels faced 95,000 Union troops in a three-day engagement that became the most famous battle of the war and produced the most casualties.

It began on July 1, 1863. After two days, the Union and Confederate armies had fought to a draw and now held opposite ridges with an open field between them. In the afternoon of the third day, General Lee ordered a daring assault that became known as Pickett's Charge, General

George Pickett being one of the Southern commanders directing the attack.

As Rebel soldiers poured onto the field, they were cut down by Union cannon and rifle fire. Those who made it across fought their way up the opposing ridge, but the Union lines held and the Southerners had to pull back. Confederate casualties were approximately 50 percent. After bracing for a Union counterattack that never came, Lee's army retreated from the field of battle in a driving rain.

Around 7,500 Union and Confederate soldiers were killed in action at Gettysburg. The number of wounded, captured, or missing exceeded 40,000 by some estimates. Although the Union victory was a turning point, it did not bring a quick end to the war. Fighting continued for two more years with almost as many casualties after the battle as before.

President Lincoln attended the dedication of a Union cemetery at Gettysburg a few months after the battle. The first speaker addressed the crowd for two hours. Lincoln followed. His Gettysburg Address lasted only a couple of minutes. He said:

> Four score and seven years ago* our fathers brought forth on this continent a new nation, conceived in liberty, and dedicated to the proposition that all men are created equal.
>
> Now we are engaged in a great civil war testing whether that nation, or any nation so conceived and so dedicated, can long endure. We are met on a great battlefield of that war. We have come to dedicate a portion of that field as a final resting place for those who here gave their lives that that nation might live. It is altogether fitting and proper that we should do this.
>
> But, in a larger sense, we can not dedicate – we can not consecrate – we can not hallow – this ground. The brave men, living and dead, who struggled here, have consecrated it, far above our poor power to add or detract. The world will little note, nor long remember what we say here, but it can never forget what they did here. It is for us the living, rather, to be dedicated here to the unfinished work which they who fought here have thus far so nobly advanced. It is rather for us to be here dedicated to the great task remaining before us – that from these honored dead we take increased devotion to that cause for which they gave the last full measure of devotion – that we here highly resolve that these dead shall not have died in vain – that this nation, under God, shall have a new birth of freedom – and that government of the people, by the people, for the people, shall not perish from the earth.

* *"Score" is another word for twenty. Four times twenty plus seven equals 87. The year referenced by Lincoln – 87 years prior to 1863 – was 1776, the year America declared independence.*

Harriet Beecher Stowe

Dred Scott

John Brown

President Abraham Lincoln

Union General Ulysses S. Grant

34-star U.S. flag during Civil War (includes stars for Confederate states)

Fugitive slaves being helped along the Underground Railroad

Fort Sumter interior after bombardment

Blockade-running Confederate steamship

C.S.A. President Jefferson Davis

Confederate General Robert E. Lee

Confederate White House in Richmond

Confederate battle flag

Ironclad battle between *Monitor* (USA) and *Merrimack* (CSA)

Rebel soldiers killed at Antietam

President Lincoln with troops near Antietam

Clara Barton, Civil War nurse, American Red Cross founder

Slaves receive news of Emancipation Proclamation

Elderly Confederate veterans reenact Pickett's Charge at 50-year reunion

General Sherman's March to the Sea

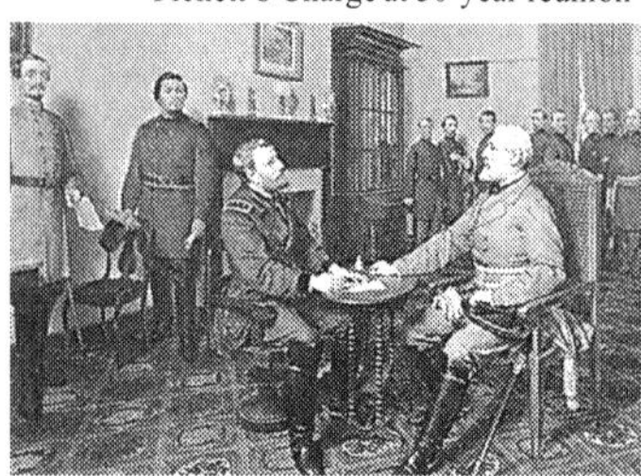
General Lee surrenders at Appomattox

Richmond after Confederate defeat

Lincoln assassination

President Andrew Johnson

Hiram Revels
First black congressman

Ku Klux Klan meeting

Former adversaries

33
MARCH TO THE SEA, APPOMATTOX, and FORD'S THEATER

On July 4, 1863, the day after the Battle of Gettysburg and a thousand miles to the southwest, 29,000 Confederate soldiers defending the heavily fortified city of Vicksburg, Mississippi, surrendered after a six-week siege. The victory gave the Union control of the entire Mississippi River and split the Confederacy in two.

The Rebels beat Union troops later that year in northern Georgia at the Battle of Chickamauga but were unable to retake Chattanooga, Tennessee, just 10 miles away. The Union's numerical and industrial superiority were becoming more apparent. The Confederacy's only hope was to exhaust the North's will to fight.

In September 1864, Union troops commanded by William Tecumseh Sherman captured the Confederate stronghold of Atlanta, Georgia, in the Deep South. General Sherman then began his "March to the Sea" to the port city of Savannah. Advancing in a wide swath, his men not only fought Confederate soldiers and destroyed railroads and bridges, they also laid waste to homes, barns, crops, and other private property in the state. Southerners resented the wanton destruction, but Sherman believed the war would end sooner if Confederate citizens as well as soldiers were convinced that the price for continuing the rebellion was too high.

In Virginia, a series of battles known as the Wilderness Campaign was fought in May and June of 1864. Pitted against each other were the two main armies in the East: the Army of the Potomac commanded by Ulysses S. Grant and the Army of Northern Virginia commanded by Robert E. Lee. Both sides won individual battles and inflicted enormous casualties, but the overall campaign was a strategic victory for the Union. It forced Lee into a defensive position to protect the Confederate capital of Richmond and the neighboring city of Petersburg. After a 10-month siege, both cities fell in early April of 1865.

General Lee escaped with his army but soon found himself hemmed in and vastly outnumbered by Union forces. Concluding that it was pointless to continue, he surrendered to General Grant on April 9 at Appomattox, Virginia. As the news spread, Confederate units in other parts of the South also gave up.* The Civil War was finally over.

The war claimed the lives of an estimated 620,000 Union and Confederate troops. As costly as the battles were, disease accounted for a majority of the deaths. Of the 470,000 soldiers who survived their wounds, many were permanently maimed. Parts of the South lay in ruins. But the war brought an end to slavery for four million blacks. It reestablished the preeminence of national interests over states' rights, settled the question of whether a state had the right to secede, and confirmed the supremacy of the Constitution and federal law over contradictory state law.

Not surprisingly, the Constitution did not address the issue of secession and reunification. President Lincoln, re-elected in 1864, formulated a lenient plan to restore the Confederate states to their place in the Union. The process, known as Reconstruction, was already underway in parts of Louisiana, Tennessee, Arkansas, and Virginia before the war ended. The Freedmen's Bureau helped reunite families and assisted former slaves with food, housing, medical care, legal matters, employment, and education. Congress passed the 13th Amendment to abolish slavery constitutionally and formally free those slaves not freed by the Emancipation Proclamation.

Less than a week after Appomattox and just six weeks into his second term, President Lincoln and his wife invited another couple to accompany them to a play at Ford's Theater, five blocks from the White House. As Lincoln and his party watched the comedy from the presidential box, John Wilkes Booth, a 26-year-old actor not involved in the performance, crept up behind the president and shot him. Booth, a Southern sympathizer, leapt down onto the stage and escaped.

President Lincoln's head wound was fatal, and he died the next morning, never regaining consciousness.† In accordance with the Constitution, Vice President Andrew Johnson, a Democrat from Tennessee and a former slaveholder, acceded to the presidency upon Lincoln's death.

Booth was killed 11 days later after he was found hiding in a Virginia barn 70 miles away. Four others implicated in the assassination were hanged after their convictions by a military tribunal.

* *The last Confederate army in Texas formally surrendered in Galveston in June 1865. On the 19th, the ranking Union general established federal control and reasserted the emancipation of the state's slaves. "Juneteenth" was made a federal holiday in 2023.*

† *Lincoln was the first president to be assassinated, but two of his predecessors also died in office. William Henry Harrison, the 9th president, died of enteric fever one month after his inauguration in 1841. Zachary Taylor, the 12th president, succumbed to severe gastroenteritis in 1850, 16 months into his term.*

34
RECONSTRUCTION and IMPEACHMENT

Andrew Johnson's Reconstruction plan, like Lincoln's, was lenient and conciliatory. The process of returning confiscated property or making restitution began.* Most Southerners who pledged allegiance to the United States and took an oath to accept the abolition of slavery were granted amnesty and had their rights as citizens restored. Large property holders and high-ranking leaders in the Confederate military and government could be pardoned only by the president.†

In the Confederate states that had not already begun Reconstruction under Lincoln, President Johnson appointed civilian provisional governors to oversee his plan. To reestablish loyal government, special elections were held in the South to select delegates to state conventions. The conventions were expected to ratify the 13th Amendment,‡ renounce any right to secession, cancel all war debts owed to their state and the Confederacy, and amend their state constitutions to include those provisions. Elections were then held for state and federal offices.

By the end of 1865, eight months after the end of the Civil War, new governments were functioning in the former Confederate states and the president, satisfied with their progress, was ready to reinstate them into the Union.

Congress objected for a number of reasons. Southerners had elected former Confederate leaders, had not allowed ex-slaves to vote, and had enacted "black codes" to perpetuate a form of slavery. For example, local sheriffs were arresting jobless blacks for vagrancy then leasing them out to white bosses to pay the fine. The codes placed constraints on when and where blacks could travel, limited employment to agriculture or domestic service, imposed restrictions on land ownership,§ and made it illegal for blacks to possess firearms or liquor, preach without a license, or fish. Former slaves were targets of violence, including lynching. Some of the perpetrators acted openly; others hid behind the cloak of secret societies such as the Ku Klux Klan (KKK).

Asserting authority over the process, Congress implemented its own Reconstruction plan. The congressional leadership refused to seat representatives and senators elected from the South under Johnson's plan. Congress passed the 14th Amendment to the Constitution that, upon ratification –

- made citizens of all persons born or naturalized in the U.S., which included former slaves¶
- prohibited states from denying equal protection of the laws or depriving citizens of their personal liberties without due process
- authorized the reduction of a state's representation in the House of Representatives in proportion to that state's denial of voting rights for adult males
- prohibited former public officials from holding office in the government or the military at the state or federal level if they had supported the rebellion after taking an oath to uphold the Constitution

- voided all debts incurred to aid the rebellion
- voided all claims for losses resulting from emancipation

Congress divided the South into five military districts, each under the control of a Union general with broad authority to oversee the congressional Reconstruction plan. Federal troops were deployed to provide enforcement if necessary. To reassume its place in the Union, a state was expected to ratify the 14th Amendment, register all adult males to vote, safeguard their voting rights, and elect delegates to a state convention to amend their state constitution again and make it acceptable to Congress.

The legislative branch remained at odds with President Johnson and in 1868 tried to oust him. The Constitution grants Congress that authority if a president is found guilty of "treason, bribery, or other high crimes and misdemeanors."

The process begins in the House of Representatives. Members draft a resolution specifying the alleged misconduct in one or more articles of impeachment. After debating the resolution, the House votes on each article or on the resolution as a whole. If even one of the articles passes by a simple majority, the president is impeached. The Senate then takes up the matter, with the chief justice of the Supreme Court presiding. Two-thirds of the Senate must concur to find the president guilty and remove him from office.

The House of Representatives impeached Andrew Johnson for trying to replace a member of his cabinet, but the Senate fell one vote short of convicting him, and he continued as president. #

A couple of months later, the United States readmitted seven of the eleven former Confederate states after they complied with the Reconstruction plan of Congress. On Christmas Day in 1868, "lame duck" President Johnson issued a blanket pardon covering everyone who had participated in the Confederate rebellion. ▲

The following year, Ulysses S. Grant succeeded Johnson as president. In 1870 the remaining Confederate states – Virginia, Mississippi, Texas, and Georgia – were readmitted to the Union after meeting an additional requirement to ratify the 15th Amendment, which made it illegal to deny voting rights based on race.

By 1877, the year usually cited as the end of Reconstruction, all the Southern states were once again fully participating in the national government, and President Rutherford B. Hayes had withdrawn the last federal troops from the South. Former slaves, most of whom registered as Republicans, were voting and serving in the U.S. Congress and in local and state offices for the first time in history. Equal rights for blacks would not come until the following century, however.

The Civil War was one of the greatest crises in American history, but the fundamental structure of the government established by the Framers survived, and the country rebounded.

* *After Robert E. Lee and his family fled south at the beginning of the war, the Union army seized their Virginia estate,* Arlington, *just across the Potomac River from Washington, D.C. The land was used as a settlement for freed slaves and a burial site for Union war dead. After the war and a long legal battle, the Supreme Court ruled that Lee's eldest son was the rightful owner. The federal government purchased the property from him in 1883 for $150,000, and it remained a national cemetery.*

† *Andrew Johnson granted 13,500 individual pardons during his presidency.*

‡ *Mississippi did not ratify the 13th Amendment until 1995.*

§ *Land ownership among former slaves remained low even after black codes were outlawed. By 1900, 35 years after the Civil War, only 25% of black farmers in the South owned the land they cultivated, while 63% of white farmers owned their land.*

To survive in the postwar economy, many Southerners turned to sharecropping. Landowners negotiated annual contracts with former slaves and poor whites to farm individual parcels for a share of what was produced. For his share (typically one-half or more), the landlord provided tools, seed, livestock, and small living quarters on the property.

¶ *In 2025, President Trump issued an executive order denying birthright citizenship to children born in the U.S. when the mother is in the country illegally or on a temporary visa and the father is not an American citizen or lawful permanent resident. The order has been challenged in federal court.*

In 1926, the Supreme Court stated that the Tenure of Office Act, the law that was the basis for Andrew Johnson's impeachment, was invalid.

▲ *A "lame duck" is someone serving out the remainder of his or her term of office after a successor has been chosen.*

35
BIG BUSINESS

The economic and industrial strength of the United States increased dramatically after the Civil War, owing to several factors:

- Deposits of oil, natural gas, coal, metal ore, and other valuable raw materials were discovered.
- Shrewd businessmen formed companies that produced and distributed goods and services efficiently.
- A burst of creativity brought a flood of inventions.
- A large and growing number of workers were available, millions of whom had emigrated from Europe and Asia.
- Electricity and the internal combustion engine provided new means of generating power.

Three industries – railroads, steel, and oil – had an enormous impact on postwar growth.

Railroads

Railroad companies in the U.S. had laid 30,000 miles of track by the year 1860. They added 163,000 more miles over the next four decades. Federal, state, and local governments subsidized some of the construction with loans and a checkerboard pattern of land grants adjacent to the tracks totaling 130 million acres, a combined area greater than the state of California.

One of the leading railroad barons of the period was Cornelius Vanderbilt. George Pullman made sleeping cars popular. Separate cars for dining and socializing made rail travel even more enjoyable.

Of all the railroad projects undertaken in the 19th century, none was more exciting or daunting than the first transcontinental railroad. Rail lines originating in the East extended only halfway across the country. The effort to bridge the 1,700-mile gap to the Pacific Coast began in 1863 during the Civil War. One company started laying track in Omaha, Nebraska, heading westward; another company started in Sacramento, California, heading eastward.

The pace intensified after the war, and in 1869 the goal was achieved when the two lines came together in Utah Territory at Promontory Summit, some 80 miles northwest of Salt Lake City. To mark the event, railroad executives used a commemorative golden spike to ceremonially fasten the last segment of track into place. The amazing accomplishment reduced coast-to-coast travel time from months to less than a week.

Reliable arrival and departure times were a necessity, but scheduling was difficult without a time standard throughout the country. Acting on their own, railroad companies implemented a plan (later adopted by the federal government) that divided the contiguous United States into four time zones exactly one hour apart. The transition took place on Sunday, November 18, 1883. As standard-time noon came to each of the zones in the country – Eastern, Central, Mountain, and Pacific – local clocks all across the zone were reset. It is remembered as "the day of two noons." *

Steel

Pennsylvania foundries forged 80 percent of the iron used by the Union military. After the war, new methods for refining iron ore made it feasible to mass produce steel, a stronger and more durable metal. Pennsylvania led the nation in steel production, and Pittsburgh was the center of the industry. Mining companies excavated iron ore in many parts of the country but found the largest deposits of high-quality ore in the Great Lakes region, particularly in northern Minnesota's Mesabi Range.

The leading figure in steel production and vertical integration in business was Andrew Carnegie. He owned not only mines and manufacturing plants but also ships and railroads used to transport his raw materials and finished goods.

Oil

Crude oil that oozed up from the ground or seeped into brine or water wells had long been considered a nuisance or, at best, a byproduct. When oil's useful properties were fully recognized, entrepreneurs dug wells specifically to extract the "black gold." Edwin Drake drilled the first commercial oil well in 1858 in Pennsylvania.[†] Other businessmen built refineries to turn the raw material into kerosene for lamps, gasoline for engines, and lubricants to make machines run smoothly.

In 1870 John D. Rockefeller founded the Standard Oil Company. By absorbing rival companies (horizontal integration) through buyouts or selling below cost if necessary to drive them out of business, he gained control of 90 percent of the petroleum refining capacity in the United States on his way to becoming America's first billionaire and the richest person in the world.

Other Industries

Textile manufacturing was at the forefront of American industrialization dating back to the 1700s. New England continued its dominance for decades after the Civil War, accounting for three-fourths of all spindles in the U.S. in 1890.[‡] Industrial sewing machines and the standardization of clothing sizes led to mass production of ready-made clothing.

Charles Pillsbury developed methods for mass producing high-quality flour. By the early 1900s, his mills were the biggest such enterprise in the world.

Philip Armour and Gustavus Swift were leaders in meatpacking. The invention of the refrigerated railroad car accelerated the growth of the industry.

Improvements to fertilizers, insecticides, plows, reapers, seed planters, and poultry incubators greatly increased agricultural output.

Business owners often needed to borrow money to start or expand large-scale operations. Many turned to J.P. Morgan, the foremost financier of the period.

* *Alaska is one hour behind Pacific Time. Hawaii is two hours behind. There has never been a rail line connecting Alaska with Canada or the lower 48 states.*

† *The modern petroleum industry began in southeastern Texas with discovery of the Spindletop oil field in 1901.*

‡ *The South would eclipse New England as the dominant textile manufacturing region by 1930.*

36
INVENTION, ENTREPRENEURS, and PHILANTHROPY

Thomas Edison was one of the greatest inventors of all time. In 1877 he built the phonograph to record and playback sound. To see if it worked, he spoke the words "Mary had a little lamb" into the machine and was surprised to hear his voice reproduced on the first attempt. Two years later, he filed a patent for the first practical electric light bulb, the invention that brought him universal fame. Edison obtained patents on a thousand other inventions, including electric generators, various types of batteries, and motion picture cameras and projectors.

Alexander Graham Bell was trying to help the hearing-impaired when he came up with the idea for the telephone. His invention, patented in 1876, would eventually replace the telegraph, a communication system developed by Samuel B. Morse that sent and received coded electrical pulses by wire.

In 1870 a woman in Reno, Nevada, paid tailor Jacob Davis \$3 to make her husband a durable pair of work pants. Davis's design using blue denim with copper rivets to reinforce the pockets was so successful locally that he asked his San Francisco fabric supplier, Levi Strauss, to partner with him to file a patent and produce the pants, later called blue jeans.

Many successful inventors and entrepreneurs started with little money or formal education and, in some cases, with no background in the field that would make them famous. Edison attended school for just three months and was thought to be unintelligent when he was young. Morse had been a portrait painter. Carnegie's first job was as a bobbin boy in a cotton mill. Rockefeller started out as a bookkeeper. Their humble beginnings inspired others to believe that anything was possible in America.

The fortunes made after the Civil War gave rise to large philanthropic contributions. Wealthy industrialists donated millions of dollars for libraries, schools, museums, hospitals, and other projects for the public good. Carnegie Hall, a prestigious music venue in New York City, is an example of such generosity.

37
CITIES

The jobs created by large and small businesses in America lured people from rural areas to cities. Urban populations also burgeoned with millions of immigrants, many of whom came to the U.S. impoverished and unable to speak English.

For immigrants arriving in New York City after 1886, the Statue of Liberty rising out of the harbor was a stirring symbol. The monument was a gift from France to commemorate the founding of the United States and celebrate the close relationship between the two countries. "The New Colossus," a poem by Emma Lazarus, is engraved on a plaque inside the pedestal. It ends with the words:

> Give me your tired, your poor,
> Your huddled masses yearning to breathe free,
> The wretched refuse of your teeming shore.
> Send these, the homeless, tempest-tossed to me,
> I lift my lamp beside the golden door!

Officials screened and processed 12 million immigrants through nearby Ellis Island beginning in 1892. Around 250,000 arrivals deemed unfit were denied entry and had to return to their countries of origin.

The rapid growth in cities put a strain on local governments and utility companies working to provide electricity, telephone service, gas for heating and cooking, police and fire protection, water and sewage systems, trash collection, and schools. Before the country fully transitioned away from horses and other animals for transportation, piles of dung had to be cleared from city streets.

The urban poor typically lived in tenements. Many of these multilevel apartment buildings were run down, overcrowded, and had few windows and no indoor plumbing. Water was available from outdoor spigots. Privies located in rear yards were pits of human waste. Better tenements had faucets in the hallways and indoor toilets shared by multiple families.

Buildings constructed of wood and built close to or connected to one another were fire hazards. A fire that swept through downtown Chicago in 1871 claimed 300 lives, destroyed thousands of structures, and left 100,000 homeless.

The throngs cramming into cities needed more indoor space, but it was also important to be near the center of town. Taller buildings were the obvious solution. The first skyscraper, built in Chicago in 1885, was 10 stories tall; subsequent high-rises had many more floors. Naturally, traffic at the ground level increased with streetcars, horse-drawn carriages, and pedestrians all competing for space on thoroughfares. To relieve congestion, large municipalities built elevated rail lines and underground subways for rapid transit through the city.

For those who could afford it, big cities offered modern household conveniences years before they were available in the rest of the country. In addition, there were art museums, theaters, orchestras, large schools and libraries, and a variety of stores and restaurants. Cities could make rural life seem dull by comparison.

38
ORGANIZED LABOR

In the latter half of the 1800s, a business owner could ignore an individual employee's demands for higher wages or better working conditions because of the seemingly endless supply of replacement workers. To give their grievances more weight, workers who all possessed a particular skill or were employed in the same industry organized into unions.* Members pay dues to support their union financially and usually have to meet certain skill requirements. They vote to determine what actions to take as a group and accept the decisions of the majority so they can act with one voice when making demands and concessions in negotiations with business owners and managers.

When management and labor cannot resolve disputes through collective bargaining, union members can try to get what they want by going on strike. During a strike, employees stop working and often form picket lines at the business, carrying signs and chanting catchy phrases stating their demands. It can be dangerous for replacement workers to cross union picket lines. A strike makes it difficult, sometimes impossible, for a company to continue operating. Vandalism is not uncommon.

The first nationwide strike occurred in 1877 after railroad companies cut employee wages. The violence that erupted left a hundred people dead, caused millions of dollars in property damage, and paralyzed rail traffic throughout the East and Midwest. This was a new age of business when disruptions at a company with extensive operations could affect people in multiple cities and states across the country.

The American Federation of Labor (AFL) was founded in 1886 as an umbrella group for various unions. It grew to become the most influential labor organization. Samuel Gompers was its first president and served in that capacity for 37 years.

* *Union membership peaked in 1945 at 35% of the nation's workforce. By 2024, it had declined to just 10%. Among private sector employees, only 6% currently belong to a union, but one-third of all government workers are unionized.*

39
THE GREAT PLAINS, INDIAN WARS, and the BUFFALO

Much of the western half of the country was still a wilderness when the Civil War began. To encourage settlement, Congress passed the Homestead Act in 1862. It granted 160 acres of public land to applicants willing to live on the property for at least five years. Anyone who had taken up arms against the U.S. was denied eligibility.

Settlers on the Great Plains encroached on the territory of the region's indigenous people, who depended on bison for their subsistence. The non-native population in the country also valued the animal, particularly for its bones (used to make fertilizers and china), hide, and tongue. The difficulty of transporting those commodities by wagon had limited the killing of bison, but with the expansion of rail lines into the Great Plains in the 1860s and '70s, an uncontrolled slaughter of the animal commenced, in some instances just for sport.

Native Americans believed they were the rightful owners of the land and fought to stop the threats to their way of life. To enforce U.S. claims and protect travelers and settlers, the government deployed the military to round up the Plains Indians and confine them to reservations.

The army's worst two defeats in these Indian wars were in the northern plains. The first took place in 1866 in Wyoming along the Bozeman Trail, which connected the gold mines of Montana with the Oregon Trail, the main overland route to the Pacific Northwest. Captain William Fetterman and the 80 men under his command encountered a small band of taunting Indians. Not realizing it was a trap, the troops chased the Indians over a ridge that concealed a thousand Lakota, Cheyenne, and Arapaho warriors. None of the soldiers survived.

Ten years later, Colonel George Armstrong Custer was riding at the head of a 600-man cavalry regiment when he came upon a large body of Native Americans camped along the Little Bighorn River in Montana. Among their chiefs were Sitting Bull and Crazy Horse. Custer divided his troops to make a three-pronged attack and personally led one of the groups. An overwhelming force, perhaps as many as 3,000 Indians, counterattacked and annihilated Custer's detachment of 210 soldiers along with 53 others from the regiment.

But it was only a matter of time before the military subdued the Plains Indians. The last major incident of armed resistance came in 1890 at Wounded Knee Creek in South Dakota. A cavalry regiment taking 300 Sioux into custody was confiscating their weapons when a gun discharged. The chaos that ensued claimed the lives of 30 soldiers and 200 Native American men, women, and children.

The traditional life of the region's indigenous people had already changed forever. The American buffalo, once numbering in the tens of millions, was near extinction. Only a thousand head remained.

In 1887 President Grover Cleveland signed the Dawes Act into law. It authorized the distribution of communally held tribal land to individual Indians on the reservations according to age and family status. Heads of households were allotted 160 acres. Unmarried persons received 80 acres if they were over 18 years old or 40 acres if they were under 18. The government granted U.S. citizenship to those receiving allotments.

If any reservation land was left over after making the allotments, the tribe could retain it or sell it to the federal government. Individuals had to keep their parcels for 25 years but could then sell. During the 47 years the law was in effect, two-thirds of Native American lands, or 103 million acres, became the property of non-Indians.

40
COWBOYS, the OPEN RANGE, and YELLOWSTONE

The extension of rail lines into Kansas after the Civil War and an increase in demand for beef made it profitable for Texas ranchers to supply cattle to meat processing plants in Chicago and elsewhere. To reach the railroad shipping points, the ranchers hired cowboys to drive their livestock hundreds of miles north over the open range. This largely unpopulated area of the Great Plains provided excellent grazing during the journey. Any unclaimed cattle found roaming on the prairie were rounded up, branded, and added to the traveling herd. The number of such animals had grown into the hundreds of thousands due to the prolonged absence of Texas ranchers and ranch hands fighting for the Confederacy.

The era of large cattle drives over the open range lasted only a couple of decades beginning around 1866. Settlers migrating to the Great Plains did not want herds passing through their land. A new invention, barbed wire, gave landowners an inexpensive fencing material to mark out property lines and create a barrier. Spikes in the twisted wire kept livestock from crossing over the fences. The well-worn cattle trails (the Chisholm, Goodnight-Loving, Western, and Shawnee) were broken up as cowboys had to make detours around private property.

The severe winter of 1886-87 and a disease transmitted to other cattle by Texas cattle ticks also contributed to the demise of the trails. Long cattle drives were no longer necessary after railroads expanding into Texas made it possible to transport the animals by rail all the way from the ranch to the packinghouse.

Gold and silver continued to lure prospectors westward. Mining towns were notorious for lawlessness and vice. Outlaws such as Butch Cassidy, Black Bart, and the Dalton Gang robbed local banks and shipments of gold, silver, and currency. Some towns survived after the mines gave out; others became ghost towns when everybody left.

With parts of the West rapidly being settled, the federal government set aside 2.2 million acres in 1872 for the first national park in the world. Yellowstone, located mostly in northwestern Wyoming, set a precedent for preserving places for their natural beauty, their historical, cultural, or environmental importance, or for recreation.*

* *Conservation would be a hallmark of Theodore Roosevelt's presidency. From 1901 to 1909, the government created five national parks, four game preserves, 24 reclamation projects, 51 bird sanctuaries, 150 national forests, and 18 national monuments – 230 million acres in all. As of 2025, there were 63 national parks in the country.*

The federal government currently controls 640 million acres, or 28% of the total 2.3 billion acres of land in the United States. Every state has some federal land within its borders. Numerous agencies administer the acreage, most of which is in the Western states. Federal lands comprise 80% of Nevada, 63% of Utah, 62% of Idaho, 61% of Alaska, 52% of Oregon, 45% of California, 2% of Texas, and .3% of Iowa.

41
EDUCATION

According to the 1870 census, 80 percent of the U.S. population over 10 years old was literate. Students attended public school an average of 78 days a year. High school enrollment was less than three percent, but enrollment in elementary schools stood at 78 percent.*

After the Civil War, enrollment at colleges and universities grew, as did the number of institutions.† Wealthy individuals such as Cornelius Vanderbilt, Ezra Cornell, and Leland Stanford founded or endowed private universities that bear their names. John D. Rockefeller's financial support helped make the University of Chicago a world-class institution.

Most institutes of higher learning were not open to women or African-Americans. After the war, more schools were established specifically for them. Smith, Wellesley, and Bryn Mawr are prestigious women's colleges founded during the period. Morehouse College and Howard University are among the oldest historically black colleges and universities (HBCU).

The Tuskegee Institute in Alabama was another prominent school for African-Americans. Its first president, Booker T. Washington, had been a slave as a child. He encouraged blacks to focus on economic advancement, and social and political equality would follow. One of Tuskegee's professors, George Washington Carver, also born into slavery, became a world-renowned scientist, agronomist, and educator.

Book publishing flourished in the postwar era. Major publishers established their corporate headquarters in New York City. Samuel Clemens, better known by his pen name, Mark Twain, was a successful author of the time. Two of his novels, *The Adventures of Tom Sawyer* (1876) and *The Adventures of Huckleberry Finn* (1884), both set in frontier America, remained popular long after their original publication.

Reading the local newspaper was a daily habit for millions of Americans. Some publishers expanded their influence by acquiring newspaper companies in multiple cities. News services such as the Associated Press (AP) made it possible for even small newspapers to report timely national and international news.

Public libraries were a familiar feature of American towns and cities by the early 1900s. Andrew Carnegie made substantial contributions toward this effort, erecting 1,700 libraries throughout the country. A college librarian, Melville Dewey, devised a decimal system that became the standard for organizing and cataloging library books.

* *The high school graduation rate reached 50% for the first time in 1940. In 2022 it was 87%.*

† *The nine chartered (degree-issuing) colleges founded in the colonial era included Harvard, Yale, and other Ivy League schools. Most were established under the auspices of certain denominations, with the education of clergy being a primary purpose. By 1860, there were 17 state universities and 229 private colleges in the country. There are currently around 4,000 colleges and universities in the United States.*

42
SPORTS

The prosperity enjoyed by most Americans in the late 19th century afforded more leisure time. For recreation, millions turned to spectator sports. Professional leagues organized games between teams from different cities. Fans filled stadiums to cheer for their home team.

Baseball, played in the summer, became the national pastime. Professional teams operated under the auspices of either the National League or the American League.* Their respective championship teams competed against each other for the first time in the 1880s. Since 1903, that contest to determine the best team in Major League Baseball has been an annual event known as the World Series.

Football, played in the fall, was first popular as a college sport beginning in the 1870s. Professional games took several decades to gain a nationwide audience.

James Naismith, a physical education instructor at the YMCA Training School in Massachusetts, needed a challenging indoor game for students during the winter months between football and baseball seasons. In 1891 he invented basketball. As originally conceived, players threw a ball into peach baskets hung at opposite ends of a gymnasium.

In the early days of professional boxing, opponents hit each other with their bare fists, and matches ended only when one of the two boxers was too injured to continue. In the late 1800s, American prizefighters adopted England's Queensberry rules, which made padded gloves mandatory. John L. Sullivan, "Gentleman Jim" Corbett, and Jack Johnson were early heavyweight champions.

* *African-Americans played in their own segregated professional baseball league for decades before Jackie Robinson broke the color barrier in the major leagues in 1947.*

43
ALASKA & HAWAII, WAR with SPAIN, and the PANAMA CANAL

In 1867 the United States purchased Alaska from the Russians for $7.2 million. Over twice the size of Texas, this additional 378 million acres increased the size of the country by 20 percent at a cost of less than 2¢ an acre. Even at that price, some people considered the acquisition a waste of money. In the years since, Alaska has proved to be worth billions in natural resources. The purchase included the Aleutian Islands, which extend out from the Alaskan mainland for 1,100 miles into the northern Pacific. Few of the 69 islands and none of the numerous islets are inhabited.

Hawaii is an archipelago consisting of more than a hundred islands spread over 1,500 miles in the central Pacific. The seven inhabited islands lie 2,500 miles southwest of California. In the 19th century, Americans and Europeans with sugar plantations in Hawaii controlled much of the economy there. In 1893 they deposed the native monarch, Queen Liliuokalani, in a bloodless coup. Five years later, the United States annexed the islands despite opposition from native Hawaiians.

By the 1890s, the Caribbean islands of Cuba and Puerto Rico and the Pacific islands of Guam and the Philippines were practically all that was left of Spain's once-vast overseas empire. American public opinion, influenced by sensationalized reporting of Spanish abuses ("yellow journalism"), favored Cuban rebels fighting for independence.

The Cuban city of Havana was a regular port of call for American naval vessels, and in January 1898 the USS *Maine* arrived. Three weeks later the battleship exploded in the harbor, killing 260 sailors. A Navy court of inquiry did not assign blame but concluded that an external marine mine had caused the disaster. It was widely believed in the U.S., though never proven conclusively, that Spaniards had sabotaged the ship.

In April 1898, the United States declared war on Spain. The Spanish-American War lasted less than four months, but America's victory produced long-term results. Cuba gained its independence,* and Puerto Rico, the Philippines, and Guam became U.S. territories.†

Admiral George Dewey was hailed as a hero for commanding a U.S. naval squadron that destroyed the Spanish fleet at the Battle of Manila Bay in the Philippines. Not one American life was lost.

The most famous soldier of the war was Theodore "Teddy" Roosevelt. After Congress declared war, he resigned his post as assistant secretary of the Navy and helped organize and lead a volunteer cavalry regiment. Known as the Rough Riders, the unit deployed for combat in Cuba. During the Battle of San Juan Hill, Roosevelt led a charge that destroyed enemy positions on an adjacent hill. His bravery catapulted him to high elective office – first as governor of New York, then as vice president, and finally as president of the United States in 1901.

Before the 20th century, the only practical sea route between the Atlantic Ocean and the Pacific was around Cape Horn, at the southern tip of South America.[‡] Digging a canal through the Isthmus of Panama, the strip of land connecting North and South America, had long been under consideration. Such a passageway through the continents would cut 8,000 miles off a voyage between New York and San Francisco.

In 1903 Colombia, which ruled Panama, rejected an American proposal to build the canal. The United States backed a revolution in Panama that enabled the people to gain their independence. The new Panamanian government accepted a treaty that gave the U.S. sovereignty over a 10-mile-wide swath of territory through the heart of the country in return for $10 million and annual payments of $250,000.

Work began the following year on what became one of the largest and most difficult engineering projects in history. The health of the workers was a major concern. American planners improved sanitation and exterminated the mosquitoes known to transmit yellow fever and malaria. In 1914 the 50-mile-long Panama Canal opened to traffic.[§]

* *During the war, the United States established a naval base (nicknamed Gitmo) at Guantanamo Bay, in southeastern Cuba, and has maintained control of the installation ever since under various treaties.*

† *The Philippines became an independent country in 1946. Of the 14 current U.S. territories, nine are uninhabitable or have small numbers of temporary residents. The five with permanent residents are:*

Caribbean	*Pacific*
Puerto Rico	*Guam*
U.S. Virgin Islands	*American Samoa*
	Northern Mariana Islands

‡ *The Northwest Passage, a continuous waterway through the North American continent, had been sought for centuries. Norwegian explorer Roald Amundsen discovered such a route in 1906, but it ran through northern Canada and was impractical for commercial navigation due to extreme cold and ice.*

§ *The U.S. maintained the Canal Zone for the rest of the century before ceding control to Panama on the last day of 1999.*

Andrew Carnegie

Pittsburgh steel mill

Carnegie library

John D. Rockefeller

Pumps bringing crude oil to the surface

J.P. Morgan

Emma Lazarus

Thomas Alva Edison

Alexander Graham Bell

Violence during 1877 railroad strike

Immigrant ship entering New York Harbor

Urban traffic

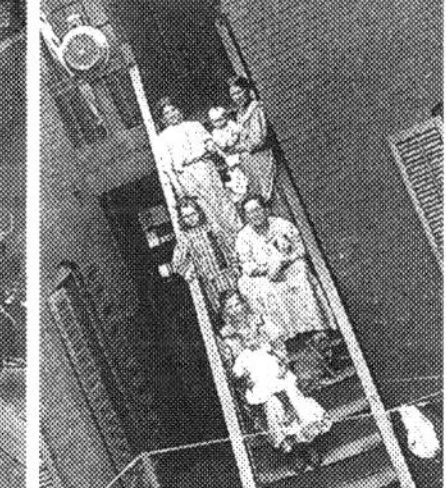
St. Louis tenement

African-American law school graduates
Howard University

Students at Women's Medical College of Pennsylvania

Completion of first transcontinental railroad

Battle of the Little Bighorn

Chief Sitting Bull

Massive pile of bison skulls

Buffalo in Yellowstone National Park

Old Faithful geyser

Cattle drive

Barbed wire fence

Homestead National Historical Park
Nebraska

Wreckage of USS *Maine*

Teddy Roosevelt & the Rough Riders

Major League Baseball

Alaska

Hawaii

Panama Canal

44
BICYCLES, AIRPLANES, and AUTOMOBILES

Bicycles had become extremely popular by the late 1800s. Millions of Americans rode for both recreation and transportation. In 1903 two bicycle mechanics invented a new type of vehicle destined to change the world.

Balloons, blimps, and dirigibles made lighter than air when filled with hot air or hydrogen or helium gas had carried people aloft before the 20th century. Pilots could control the flight of such aircraft to a certain extent and land safely, but the principles of modern aerodynamics were not known. In 1899 Wilbur and Orville Wright, owners of a small but successful bicycle shop in Dayton, Ohio, set out to solve those mysteries, which had perplexed scientists, engineers, and inventors for centuries.

After reading everything they could find on the subject, the brothers built kites and gliders to conduct their own experiments, most of which took place at Kill Devil Hills, a remote coastal village on North Carolina's Outer Banks. With strong winds blowing in off the ocean, high dunes from which to launch, and the somewhat-forgiving beach sand when they landed hard, it was an ideal location.

After two years of toil, the obstacles still seemed insurmountable. A discouraged Wilbur said it would be 50 years before man ever flew. But they kept working, and breakthroughs came the following year. By 1902, they had mastered the principles of flight in their glider. To achieve powered flight, they needed a strong but lightweight motor and highly efficient propellers. When those could not be found, the two were again forced to rely on their own research and skill. They designed and built the motor and propellers themselves.

Their airplane was ready on the morning of December 17, 1903. The weather was cold and windy at Kill Devil Hills. With Orville at the controls and his older brother running alongside, the plane rose from a flat stretch of beach to make the world's first powered, controlled, and sustained flight of a heavier-than-air flying machine. It lasted 12 seconds and covered a distance of 40 yards. On the fourth and final flight of the day, Wilbur stayed aloft for 59 seconds and flew 284 yards.

Although none of the flights went higher than 15 feet or faster than 10 miles per hour groundspeed, they were a triumph of Yankee ingenuity. The inventors telegraphed news of their achievement from the nearby town of Kitty Hawk. It was so unimaginable that, for years, many people refused to believe eyewitness accounts that the Wright brothers could indeed fly.

In ground transportation, improvements to the internal combustion engine spurred innovation to replace the horse and buggy with a motorized vehicle, or "horseless carriage." Henry Ford emerged as the most successful automobile manufacturer. His hometown of Detroit, Michigan, already a commercial and transportation hub, became the center of the industry.

The Ford Motor Company began making cars in 1903, but production costs were so high that only the wealthy could buy the vehicles. That changed after Ford started using assembly lines. A car was built by different groups of workers as the chassis was conveyed down a track running the length of the plant. One group installed the engine, another group the wheels, and so on, until a completed car rolled off the end of the line, ready for sale.

Assembly lines and other innovative and efficient manufacturing techniques lowered Ford's production costs so dramatically that he was able to sell his Model T at a price most households could afford. The cars came in only one color: black. Sales skyrocketed, but workers at Ford factories struggled with the monotony of performing repetitive tasks. To maintain morale and reduce employee turnover, he shortened their workday from nine hours to eight and more than doubled the wage of the average autoworker to the unprecedented sum of $5 a day (equal to $162 today).

By 1917, Ford and other manufacturers had sold close to seven million motor vehicles in the United States. Towns advertised to attract tourists, and businesses catering to travelers sprang up along the highways. Federal, state, and local governments had difficulty building and maintaining roads to accommodate the ever-increasing traffic.

45
PICTURES and RADIO

The first cameras were bulky and hard to operate, even for professionals. Still images were captured on flat metal or glass plates. In 1888 George Eastman's company, Kodak, made picture-taking possible for amateurs by producing a small box camera that used flexible roll film. When Kodak introduced its Brownie camera in 1900 for just $1, photography became available to virtually everyone.

A related industry was born with the invention of cameras that recorded motion and projectors that displayed those images on wide screens for large audiences. Movies in the early days were filmed in black and white and had no sound ("silent movies"), but people flocked to theaters, which sprang up all over the country.*

Filmmakers built the first motion picture studios in the Northeast and Midwest, but those were not suitable locations during the winter months, when harsh weather made shooting outdoor scenes difficult, if not impossible. Movie producers found an ideal climate in the Southern California town of Hollywood. The relocation was also prompted by Edison's vigorous enforcement of his film equipment patents back East.

Radio, an even bigger form of mass media, made wireless transmission into homes possible. By the 1920s, competing companies were producing news and entertainment programs to attract listeners and advertisers. Broadcasts were free to anyone within range of the radio signal.

* *Movies with spoken dialogue ("talkies") were introduced in the 1920s. By the '30s, music, sound effects, and color were additional features incorporated into commercially successful films.*

46
PROGRESSIVISM

Industrial growth after the Civil War fueled a rise in the standard of living, and some people amassed huge fortunes, but significant societal problems developed. Mark Twain called the era a Gilded Age, not a golden one. The wealth that was created masked the struggles of those less fortunate. "Muckraking" journalists sought to expose the ills: the power of monopolies, the plight of the poor, the mistreatment of workers, and the selling of harmful products. Progressivism, the movement to correct these and other problems, rejected laissez-faire capitalism in favor of increased government intervention.

Monopolies and trusts were large companies whose business methods or dominance in a particular market inhibited competition. Congress passed the Sherman Antitrust Act in 1890 and the Clayton Antitrust Act in 1914 to break up monopolies and keep new ones from forming. The enforcement of these laws was known as "trustbusting." The government created the Interstate Commerce Commission and the Federal Trade Commission to monitor business practices and encourage competition.

The decennial census in the year 1900 counted approximately two million children as laborers. Some held jobs instead of going to school. Children could be found working long hours and even through the night in unsafe conditions. The federal government passed legislation in 1916 and 1919 to address the problem, but the Supreme Court struck down those laws as unconstitutional.*

The Jungle, a popular 1906 novel by Upton Sinclair, sensationalized unsanitary conditions in the meatpacking industry. The public outcry led to passage of the Pure Food and Drug Act, which made it unlawful to manufacture, sell, or distribute food products or medicines that were harmful or did not have accurate labels on the packaging.

In 1912, voters elected Woodrow Wilson as the nation's 28th president. He had been governor of New Jersey and president of Princeton University and is the only U.S. president to hold a PhD (in political science).

President Wilson urged legislators to reduce tariffs and levy a tax on individual incomes. The country's first income tax, imposed in 1862 during the Civil War, lasted only 10 years. Congress revived the tax in 1894, but the Supreme Court declared it unconstitutional. The 16th Amendment, ratified in 1913, removed the constitutional obstacle, and later that year, the federal government instituted a tax on personal incomes.† A tax on corporate incomes had been levied four years earlier. Income taxes have been a permanent fixture of the U.S. tax code ever since and currently account for over half of all federal revenue. The Internal Revenue Service (IRS), a bureau of the Treasury Department, enforces the tax statutes.

Personal income taxes are progressive, meaning the tax rate increases as income rises. In other words, individuals with higher taxable incomes generally pay a greater percentage of their income in taxes, up to a maximum rate.‡

Wilson also signed the Federal Reserve Act into law in 1913. The legislation revamped currency laws and instituted a central banking system with 12 regional federal banks. The Federal Reserve exercises broad powers in controlling credit and regulating the flow of money. As the "lender of last resort," it can provide emergency loans to financial institutions to help stabilize the economy during a crisis. The agency is subject to congressional oversight, but by and large, it is an independent body within the U.S. government.

* *In 1938, federal lawmakers passed the Fair Labor Standards Act, and the courts upheld its restrictions on child labor.*

† *Since 1943, the federal government has collected personal income taxes primarily through payroll deductions. Employers are required to withhold a specified amount from each employee's paycheck based on the worker's wages, married status, number of dependents, etc. The company remits the money to the IRS, which applies it to the employee's estimated annual tax liability. Individuals must calculate the exact amount owed for the year and submit the results on forms designed by the government. The deadline for filing personal income tax returns for the prior year is April 15. If taxpayers owe more, they must pay the additional amount by that date to avoid a penalty. If too much tax was withheld, the Department of the Treasury refunds the difference to the employee. Most states impose a separate state income tax.*

‡ *In 2025, the corporate income tax rate was 21%. The highest personal income tax rate was 37%. The wealthiest 5% typically pay around 60% of the federal personal income taxes collected. According to the Tax Policy Center, 40% of those filing tax returns (76 million households), most of whom are at the lower income levels, paid no federal income tax. In 1990, the percentage of filers who paid no federal income tax was 21%.*

47

WORLD WAR I

Events in Europe overshadowed progressive reforms in America. Austria-Hungary had annexed Bosnia in 1908. When the Austrian archduke, Francis Ferdinand, and his wife visited Bosnia in 1914, they were assassinated by a Serbian revolutionary. Austria-Hungary declared war on Serbia. As other nations honored their alliances, the situation cascaded until most of the continent and eventually much of the world was at war. On one side were the Allies, which included Serbia, France, Britain, Russia, Italy, and Japan. Their enemies, known as the Central Powers, were Austria-Hungary, Germany, Turkey, and Bulgaria. For the first years of the war, the U.S. remained officially neutral, although American firms favored the Allies in terms of exports and bank loans.

When neither side could gain the upper hand on the battlefield, the armies dug protective trenches opposite each other along a 500-mile front from the Belgian coast to the Swiss border. Soldiers ventured out of their trenches only sporadically to cross the "no man's land" and attack the other side's trenches. Charging the enemy, a common tactic in earlier wars, was much more dangerous in World War I* because of land mines, barbed wire, and machine guns that could fire continuously.

To break the stalemate, the combatants introduced poison gas as a weapon. The gases caused burns and blisters on the skin, blindness upon contact with the eyes, and death if inhaled. With enough warning, a soldier could survive such an attack by donning a gas mask, but serious injury was still possible.

The British invented the tank, an armored track vehicle that could cross over barbed wire and trenches to fire on opposing troops. Airplanes built for warfare shot down military balloons and dirigibles, carried out bombing and reconnaissance missions, and engaged in aerial "dogfights" with enemy fighter planes.

At sea, both sides tried to keep supplies from getting through to their adversaries. Germany's use of submarines, or "undersea boats," was extremely effective. U-boats could launch torpedoes and submerge without ever being seen. Deck guns gave them the capability of attacking from the surface. U-boats were dreaded weapons that sent close to 5,000 Allied and neutral ships to the bottom of the ocean.

In 1915 an English ocean liner, the *Lusitania*, was returning from New York when it went down off the coast of Ireland, sunk by a single U-boat torpedo. Twelve hundred passengers, including 128 Americans, died in the attack. The German government expressed regret for the loss of life but defended the action because the liner's cargo included munitions destined for use against German troops.

Americans were outraged. To mollify the U.S., Germany pledged not to target passenger ships in the future but maintained the right to search merchant vessels. If war materiel were found, a ship might be confiscated or sunk, but non-combatants would not be harmed.

Diplomacy kept the U.S. out of the war for the time being. Americans did not want to become more involved in a faraway conflict. The Atlantic Ocean served as a protective buffer. Nevertheless, the United States prepared to enter the war if necessary.†

Germany's efforts to form an alliance with Mexico against the U.S. came to light in January 1917. In February, Germans reneged on their earlier pledge and returned to unrestricted submarine warfare, sinking several American merchant ships over the next two months. President Wilson went to Capitol Hill in April seeking a declaration of war to make the world "safe for democracy." Congress declared war on Germany a few days later. War was declared on Austria-Hungary in December. The United States did not declare war on the other Central Powers. Turkey and Bulgaria were not seen as direct threats, and the U.S. did not want to jeopardize its relations in the region.

* *At the time, the conflict was called the Great War because many countries and millions of troops were engaged. After war broke out across the world again in 1939, it became more common to refer to the Great War as World War I.*

† *U.S. preparations included the $25 million purchase of the Danish Virgin Islands in 1916 to prevent Germany from acquiring those Caribbean islands for a naval base.*

48
MOBILIZATION and ARMISTICE

Since the Founding, Americans had opposed having a large standing military when not at war. Consequently, troop strength in 1916 was under 200,000. After declaring war the following year, Congress instituted a draft to quickly build up a force of sufficient size. The U.S. conscripted 2.7 million men into the armed services. With the addition of volunteers, National Guard troops, and reservists called up to active duty, nearly five million Americans served in the First World War.

Production in the United States shifted to the war effort. The federal government set maximum prices (ceilings) for industrial products such as steel and rubber. Food supplies, as essential as military equipment, were increased by admonishing the public to avoid waste, plant "victory gardens," and curtail consumption. High minimum prices (floors) mandated for wheat encouraged farmers to grow more.

Getting raw materials and manufactured goods delivered when and where needed was a huge task. The government ordered the construction of more rail cars and locomotives and temporarily put the railroads under federal control to keep freight from getting bogged down in competing rail lines. Transporting soldiers, equipment, and supplies across the Atlantic to the war zone was a bigger problem. More ships were built. To get past enemy U-boats, cargo vessels and troop transports sailed close together in convoys escorted by warships.

Troops of the American Expeditionary Force (AEF) commanded by General John J. Pershing began arriving in France in June 1917. They provided a great boost to demoralized Allied soldiers facing an influx of German troops from the Eastern Front after Russia withdrew from the conflict. The Central Powers launched a series of attacks the following spring hoping to win the war before more Americans, nicknamed "Yanks" or "Doughboys," could be brought up. German troops got to within 50 miles of Paris before they were stopped. In ferocious combat at Belleau Wood, U.S. Marines had to use knives, shovels, and even their bare fists to beat the enemy back.

Later in 1918, more than a million Americans were engaged along the Meuse-Argonne front, part of a larger Allied offensive. Fighting in rugged terrain, heavy fog, and rain, U.S. troops defeated a large part of the German army by cutting off a vital railroad supply line and overcoming some of the most heavily fortified positions on the Western Front. The armies of the Central Powers collapsed. Germany, the last to give up, agreed to an armistice, or cessation of fighting, that went into effect at the 11th hour on the 11th day of the 11th month (November).

More than 116,000 U.S. servicemen died in the war, and 204,000 were wounded. Their sacrifice made the Allied victory possible. Worldwide, at least 15 million died, counting civilians and military personnel.

After the fighting stopped, the heads of the victorious Allied nations met to draft separate terms of surrender for each of the Central Powers. President Wilson had already formulated 14 policies he believed would bring about a lasting peace. Some thought the Great War would be "the war to end all wars," but the extremely punitive Treaty of Versailles with Germany signed by Wilson and the other Allied leaders sowed the seeds of a much more destructive global conflict just two decades later. The treaty placed total responsibility for the war on the Central Powers, obligated Germans to pay steep reparations to compensate the Allies for their losses, and forced Germany to give up all of its overseas colonies and a sizeable portion of its territory in Europe. The German people bitterly resented the terms.

The last of Wilson's "14 Points" was written into the Treaty of Versailles and called for the creation of an international body to resolve disputes. The League of Nations met regularly from 1920 to 1946, but the United States never joined, and the U.S. Senate did not ratify the treaty.

In the aftermath of the war, much of the world's political map had to be redrawn, and millions of people were displaced or found themselves living under a different government.

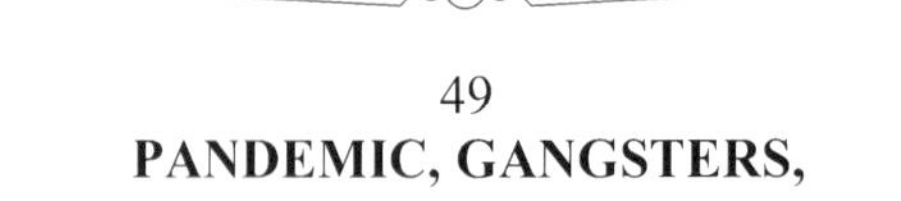

49
PANDEMIC, GANGSTERS, SUFFRAGISTS, and IMMIGRATION

A flu virus in 1918 and 1919 spread across the globe in one of the worst pandemics in history, taking even more lives than World War I. A quarter of the U.S. population, some 25 million people, contracted the disease, and 675,000 Americans died – 196,000 in the month of October 1918 alone. Many succumbed within hours of becoming infected. Young and middle-aged adults showed an unusually high susceptibility.

A period known as Prohibition began in 1919 with ratification of the 18th Amendment, which banned the manufacture, sale, or distribution of alcoholic beverages. Those who ignored the law were called bootleggers. Some outlaws involved in bootlegging and other illegal activities banded together and maintained their criminal enterprises through bribery, extortion, and murder. Al Capone, based in Chicago, was one of the most notorious gangsters of the period.*

In 1920, the Constitution was amended again. The 19th Amendment prohibited the denial or abridgement of voting rights (also called suffrage or the franchise) based on sex. The push to secure that right and others for women began before the Civil War and was an outgrowth of the fight to abolish slavery. Lucretia Mott and Elizabeth Cady Stanton were among the leaders who organized the first women's rights convention at Seneca Falls, New York, in 1848. Other reformers such as Susan B. Anthony, Carrie Chapman Catt, and Alice Paul advanced the movement that eventually achieved universal female suffrage in the U.S.†

The number of immigrants coming to the United States from southern and eastern Europe rose dramatically after the turn of the century. It spawned a backlash and a rise in nativism, the favoring of existing residents over newcomers. In 1921, President Warren G. Harding signed the Emergency Quota Act, the nation's first quantitative immigration law. It limited the annual number of new immigrants of any nationality to three percent of their foreign-born countrymen already residing in the U.S. The government made exceptions for children of American citizens and immigrants from the Western Hemisphere.

Two hundred thousand African-Americans served abroad in the military during the First World War. They returned home seeking greater opportunity in society and wanting the same respect they had received from foreigners. The revived Ku Klux Klan used violence, including murder, to keep that from happening. The KKK also targeted Catholics and Jews. Meeting at night in ritualistic outdoor gatherings, Klan members dressed in white robes, wore hoods to hide their faces, and burned crosses.

Southern blacks in large numbers had begun relocating to cities in the North prior to World War I. That trend continued after the war. From 1910 to 1930, more than a million people were part of this Great Migration. The transition was often difficult due to low-paying jobs, racism, and housing in run-down neighborhoods. Race riots flared up in several Northern cities, most notably in East St. Louis, Illinois, in 1917.

* *Prohibition ended in 1933 with ratification of the 21st Amendment, which repealed the 18th Amendment.*

† *Some U.S. states and territories allowed women to vote prior to the 19th Amendment.*

50
THE JAZZ AGE

The 1920s are often called the Roaring Twenties or the Jazz Age. Jazz, a uniquely American musical genre that became popular in the decade, grew out of the spirituals and work songs of slaves. Singer Bessie Smith and composer, pianist, and band leader Duke Ellington were early pioneers. The Charleston was a dance inspired by the music.

Art Deco, a style of art and design marked by clean lines, geometric motifs, and shiny surfaces, influenced everything from architecture to furniture to trains. Glass, metal, and fine wood were often incorporated.

The author who best symbolized the period was F. Scott Fitzgerald. The literary world also recognized Ernest Hemingway and William Faulkner as important figures. The playwright Eugene O'Neill won three Pulitzer Prizes in the decade. Two magazines first published in the Twenties, *Reader's Digest* and *Time*, still have wide circulations.

In 1927 American aviator Charles Lindbergh became an international hero by making the first nonstop transatlantic flight between New York and Paris. The 3,600-mile journey took 33½ hours in his small single-engine airplane, the *Spirit of St. Louis*, and earned him a $25,000 prize.*

The overall U.S. economy grew in the '20s, but serious problems developed. Farm incomes declined because of overproduction and a drop in foreign demand for American agricultural goods after World War I. Businesses and individuals took on too much debt. Banks and brokerages overextended themselves with risky loans, some of which were used to speculate in the stock market, where shares of publicly traded companies are bought and sold. There are a number of facilities for trading stocks in the United States. The largest is the New York Stock Exchange, located on Wall Street in New York City.

When people buy stock or shares in a company, they become part-owners, although the individual percentage of ownership is usually small. Shareholders make a profit if the company pays dividends† or if the stock sells for more than the purchase price. A loss is realized when shares sell for less than the purchase price. A stock's price often drops if company revenues or profits do not meet expectations, but other factors can affect the value as well.

In the 1920s, investors bid share prices to record highs. The Dow Jones Industrial Average, an important stock market index, multiplied in value by a factor of six during the decade.

* *In 1935 Amelia Earhart made the first solo flight between Hawaii and California, the longest stretch of open ocean in the world. The 2,400-mile trip took just over 18 hours.*

† *cash payments made by a company to its shareholders*

51
THE GREAT DEPRESSION

Market economies are cyclical; they expand and contract. Over the course of the long-term upward trend, the U.S. economy experienced several severe downturns in the 19th century beginning in 1807, 1837, 1873, and 1893, respectively. Each depression lasted for years.

The worst contraction of all, the Great Depression, occurred in the 20th century and persisted for a decade. It began in October 1929 when plummeting stock prices spread panic across the country. Consumers cut back on purchases. Businesses laid off workers* or reduced the wages of those kept on the payroll. There was a "run" on banks as bank customers, in need of cash and worried about the security of their deposits, tried to withdraw all their money. Many banks ran out of cash.

Banks do not keep on hand all the money their customers deposit. Most of it is loaned out to businesses and individuals and invested in stocks, bonds, and other securities. Like everyone else with stock market investments, banks lost money in the crash. On top of that, bank customers defaulted on loans. Unable to withstand such reversals, 9,100 banks, a third of the total in the country, went out of business between 1929 and 1933.

Families lost homes when they could no longer pay their mortgages. In some cities, the homeless set up shacks in empty fields. Those who blamed President Herbert Hoover for the bad economy called these shantytowns "Hoovervilles." People in large cities who did not have money to buy food stood in long lines to get free meals of soup and bread provided by charities and the government.

In general, the federal government responded poorly to the crisis, increasing its severity and duration. The Federal Reserve did not shore up the banking system when the money supply was contracting. Taxes were increased. High tariffs inhibited foreign trade.

Entertainment helped people cope with the challenges. Americans listened to radio programs and music recordings. With ticket prices as low as 10¢, movies remained popular during the hard times.

* *The unemployment rate during the Great Depression peaked in 1933 at 25% of the labor force and was still high, 19%, in 1938.*

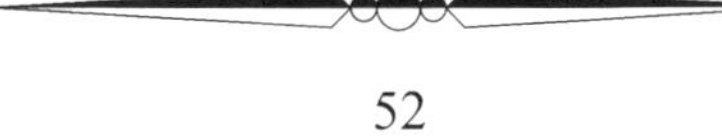

52
NEW DEAL

The presidential election of 1932 came three years into the Great Depression. Franklin Delano Roosevelt, a distant cousin of Teddy Roosevelt, soundly defeated President Hoover. Often referred to by his initials, FDR told the nation in his inaugural address that "the only thing we have to fear is fear itself." In "fireside chats" broadcast over the radio, President Roosevelt tried to reassure Americans that the worst was behind them and the government was working to help solve the nation's problems. His optimism was contagious. The fact that he had polio and could not walk was not widely publicized.*

Under Roosevelt's plan, called the New Deal, the federal government implemented a flurry of programs and economic reforms.

There was widespread distrust of banks because people had lost money when their banks failed.† The president signed legislation creating the Federal Deposit Insurance Corporation (FDIC), an agency that guarantees the safety of customer bank accounts up to specified limits.

Investors were the first to be hurt by the economic collapse.‡ To rebuild trust in the financial markets, the Securities and Exchange Commission (SEC) was created to regulate stock and bond transactions and punish fraud.

To reduce unemployment, the federal government funded and managed public works projects such as the construction of roads, bridges, schools, airports, hospitals, parks, and housing for the poor. The Tennessee Valley Authority (TVA) was created to build dams for flood control and to harness waterpower for cheaper electricity in the South. Out West, the Hoover Dam was completed on the Colorado River and construction began on the Grand Coulee Dam on the Columbia River.

The government paid farmers to grow less and, in some cases, to destroy existing farm produce and livestock. The reduction in supply caused food prices to rise, which increased farm incomes. Farmers also benefited from the extension of electrical power to rural areas.

The Great Depression was especially trying for farmers on the Great Plains. The soil had deteriorated due to shortsighted agricultural practices and a drought that began in 1931. Strong winds that blew across the Plains states carried away the topsoil in giant dust storms that left much of the region a "Dust Bowl" unsuitable for farming. Many families had no alternative but to pack up and move.

The federal government enacted Social Security in 1935 to provide retirement benefits to workers. Later, the disabled and certain surviving members of a deceased worker's family also received payments under the program.[§]

In 1938 Congress passed a labor law that reduced the standard workweek to 40 hours, guaranteed a minimum wage of 25¢ an hour, set minimum ages for employment, and limited the hours minors could work.

* *Vaccines developed by Jonas Salk and Albert Sabin would virtually eliminate polio in the U.S. by the 1960s.*

† *Customers of failed banks lost an average of 20¢ of every dollar they had on deposit.*

‡ *The stock market bottomed out in 1932 at 11% of its 1929 high. The market did not recover its value lost in the Great Depression until 1954, 25 years after the crash.*

§ *Social Security benefits, often called entitlements, are available to most people when they reach the standard retirement age of 66 (62 for early retirement). The expenditures account for 23% of the federal budget. To fund the program, the government assesses a 12.4% tax on payrolls and self-employment income. The tax burden is borne equally by employers and employees. The employee's share is deducted from each paycheck at 6.2% of gross earnings. Self-employed individuals pay both halves. Due to the aging U.S. population, the ratio of contributors to beneficiaries is currently 2.7 to 1. In 2025, 67 million Americans were receiving monthly benefit checks.*

Social Security started out as a pay-as-you-go system with the tax rate being raised periodically to keep pace with disbursements. In anticipation of the large baby boom generation reaching retirement age, President Reagan signed legislation in 1983 to overhaul the system. The tax rate was increased to create a reserve. That trust fund grew every year because the taxes collected, together with the interest earned on the accumulated reserve, were greater than the benefits paid out. In 2010, the payouts began to exceed the taxes collected, but the interest more than made up for the shortfall, and the fund kept growing. Starting in 2021, however, the interest was no longer enough to cover the deficit, and the reserve had to be tapped. According to government projections, the Social Security trust fund will be depleted by 2034.

First successful powered flight – Wright brothers

Henry Ford with Model T

Silent movie poster

Early home radio

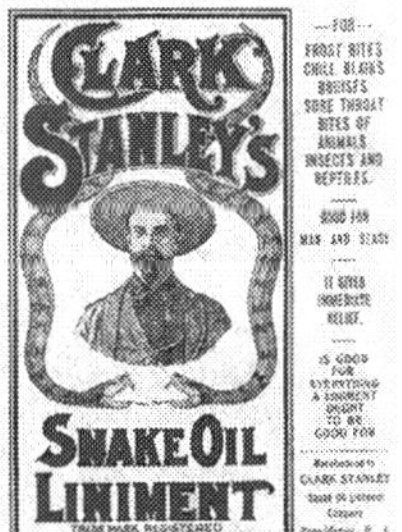

Fake medicine

Child at work in textile mill

IRS logo

Uncle Sam poster

Soldiers in gas masks

World War I trench warfare

Flu epidemic hospital

Banned alcohol poured down sewer

Suffragists

Art Deco
Chrysler Building

Roaring '20s fashion

Charles Lindbergh

Bessie Smith

Duke Ellington

Family relocating during Great Depression

Free food for the unemployed

FDR broadcasts fireside chat

Plains dust storm

Social Security card

Hoover Dam

Japanese attack on Pearl Harbor

Women building a B-24 bomber

D-Day

Nazi concentration camp

Air power

Naval strength

Marines on Iwo Jima

Atomic bombing of Nagasaki

Americans celebrate end of World War II

Europe rebuilds with Marshall Plan

53
WORLD WAR II

In the latter half of the 1930s, the specter of another world war loomed. Italy attacked Ethiopia in 1935. Two years later, the Empire of Japan went to war with China. The most ominous threat emerged in Germany, where Adolph Hitler's National Socialist (Nazi) party gained control of the government and rebuilt the military. In fiery speeches, Hitler fanned the resentment Germans felt about their treatment after World War I and called for revenge. He told ethnic Germans they were a superior Aryan race* destined to rule the world for a thousand years. He incited hatred and persecution of Jews, who were terrorized, rounded up and incarcerated, or killed.

In 1936 Hitler violated the Treaty of Versailles by sending troops into the Rhineland. This German region along the Rhine River was supposed to remain free of militarization after World War I and serve as a buffer between the rest of Germany and neighboring countries to the west, but Allied nations acquiesced to the incursion.

Over the next three years, Germany annexed Austria, the Sudetenland (a part of Czechoslovakia inhabited by ethnic Germans), and then all of Czechoslovakia. Diplomatic efforts to halt the aggression ended in September of 1939 when Germany invaded Poland. Britain, France, and other countries, finally convinced that Hitler could be stopped only by force, declared war on Germany. World War II had begun.

In lightning attacks (*blitzkrieg*), the German military (*Wehrmacht*) stormed across the continent. Denmark, Norway, Holland, Belgium, and Luxembourg quickly fell to the onslaught. Germany's ally and fellow fascist state, Italy, helped in a minor way to defeat France. By the summer of 1940, most of the European mainland was under German or Italian control.

Hitler set his sights across the English Channel. He believed his air force (*Luftwaffe*) could bomb England into submission or weaken the country's defenses before invading with ground troops. The frightening air raids lasted nearly a year and killed 43,000 civilians, but British Prime Minister Winston Churchill vowed never to surrender. The outnumbered Royal Air Force lost 500 pilots and 1,000 planes in the Battle of Britain, but Germany lost 2,700 airmen and 1,900 planes. Hitler canceled his plans for an amphibious invasion.

The United States did not enter the war for two years after it began. Most Americans were isolationists, but those sentiments gradually changed as the international situation worsened.

President Roosevelt prepared the country to assume a leading role and be "the great arsenal of democracy." In 1940 he persuaded Congress to pass the first conscription bill in U.S. history when the nation was not at war. In March of the following year, he ordered the seizure of German and Italian ships docked in American ports. That same month, Congress passed the Lend-Lease Act authorizing the president to provide arms and other aid to countries whose defense was considered vital to the United States. American ships transporting the materiel abroad and naval escorts providing protection risked being attacked.

In June of 1941, Germany invaded the Soviet Union† in violation of their mutual non-aggression pact. America responded to this major escalation of the war by sending aid to Russia, but it would be an event later that year in the Pacific, not Europe, that drew the United States into the war as a combatant.

* *a supposed master race of non-Jewish Caucasians ideally having Nordic features*

† *After communist revolutionaries toppled the Russian monarchy in 1917 during World War I, new governments arose in the various regions of the former empire. In 1922 they came together to form a new nation, the Union of Soviet Socialist Republics (U.S.S.R.), also known as the Soviet Union or Russia, the largest republic.*

54
PEARL HARBOR

Japan, an island nation lacking many critical natural resources, had to import raw materials and equipment to provide for its military. American firms supplied 80 percent of the country's oil needs. Japan's continued aggression in Asia prompted the U.S. to restrict the sale of arms and other strategic goods in 1940. When Japan formed an alliance with Germany and Italy, the United States sent military aid to China under the Lend-Lease program. After Japanese troops moved into southern Indochina in July 1941, President Roosevelt froze Japanese assets in America and cut off oil sales.

The strained relations were severed on Sunday, December 7, 1941, when carrier-based Japanese planes struck five U.S. military installations in Hawaii, in particular, the naval base at Pearl Harbor. The two-hour raid killed 2,335 troops and 68 civilians and left 1,178 wounded. Fortunately, nine out of ten sailors were on shore leave and not aboard their ships, the dry docks and a depot storing 4½ million gallons of fuel remained intact, and no aircraft carrier was in port, but the attack damaged or destroyed 21 other ships and 347 aircraft. The president called it "a date which will live in infamy." Congress declared war on Japan the next day and declared war on Germany and Italy three days later.

Citizens of Japan, Germany, and Italy who were in the United States were immediately designated by Roosevelt as "alien enemies" subject to detention. Two months later, he issued an executive order authorizing the relocation and internment of anyone the military deemed a possible threat. Ethnic Japanese along the U.S. Pacific coast bore the brunt of the policy. Around 112,000 were uprooted and confined to remote camps farther inland during the war; 70,000 were U.S. citizens.* For a time, Japanese-Americans were barred from enlisting in the military. Many of those already serving had their weapons taken away and were reassigned to segregated units and given menial tasks.†

* *In 1948 the federal government paid some compensation to those affected by the internment policy. President Reagan signed legislation in 1988 that formally apologized for the government's actions and gave $20,000 to surviving internees.*

† *The government modified its policies, and 33,000 Japanese-Americans eventually served in World War II. Many saw combat, mostly in segregated units in Europe, and 800 gave their lives. One of those units, the army's highly decorated 442nd Regimental Combat Team, produced 21 Medal of Honor recipients during the war. The group's motto was "Go for broke."*

55
ALLIES versus AXIS

The "Big Three" Allied nations that fought in World War II were the United States, Great Britain, and the U.S.S.R. Their respective leaders were Roosevelt, Churchill, and Joseph Stalin. Hitler, Benito Mussolini, and Emperor Hirohito were the leaders of Germany, Italy, and Japan, the main enemy or Axis countries.

The war was fought in two large geographic areas or theaters – against the Japanese in Asia and the Pacific islands (Pacific Theater), and against the Germans and Italians in North Africa and Europe (European Theater). The Allies made defeating Germany the top priority.

Industrial production in the U.S. increased dramatically to support the war. Americans donated household metal, paper products, and rubber to be recycled into military supplies. The government instituted wage and price controls and imposed a moratorium on the manufacture of cars, appliances, and other non-essential consumer items. Essential goods were rationed based on need. To purchase meat, sugar, canned food, shoes, or gas, citizens had to present a government-issued coupon to the seller.

The urgent need for military personnel and equipment brought an end to the unemployment problem that had plagued the U.S. for a decade. Businesses recruited women, a "hidden army," to fill positions vacated by men going off to war.* Incomes rose. Congress raised taxes to help pay for increased military spending, but even with that, Americans had extra money and much of it went into savings accounts and war bonds, personal loans to the government to help finance the war.

German submarines hampered the buildup of Allied forces in the European Theater. Often working in coordinated groups or "wolf packs," U-boats sank 3,000 ships, many of them in the Gulf of America, the Caribbean, and along the U.S. East Coast. Lighting in coastal communities was restricted at night to keep ships from being silhouetted for U-boat attackers. The Allies armed their merchant ships, increased the number of airplanes and warships escorting convoys across the Atlantic, and outfitted naval vessels with sonar, a technology used to find submerged submarines. Radar and intercepted German radio transmissions helped planes and ships locate U-boats when they surfaced. Hitler was unaware that the Allies had deciphered Enigma, Germany's secret code used to encrypt messages. These measures lessened the U-boat threat. In addition, the United States built two massive pipelines from Texas to the Northeast to transport vital oil and gas underground instead of by sea.

In November 1942, U.S. forces joined the Allies already fighting in North Africa. They drove out the Germans and Italians the following year. Attention then turned to the liberation of Europe, which began with an Allied invasion of Italy. The fighting was especially fierce at the Anzio beachhead, but early in June of 1944, the Allies liberated Rome from the Germans. Italians had already deposed Mussolini, and the new government had switched Italy's allegiance to the Allies.

* *More than 350,000 women enlisted in the U.S. military during World War II and served in every branch. They were nurses, clerks, pilots, gunnery instructors, cryptologists, truck drivers, and mechanics. Most were stationed in the States, and those who went overseas received non-combat assignments. Nevertheless, 432 female service members died, 16 due to enemy action. Eighty-eight were held as prisoners of war.*

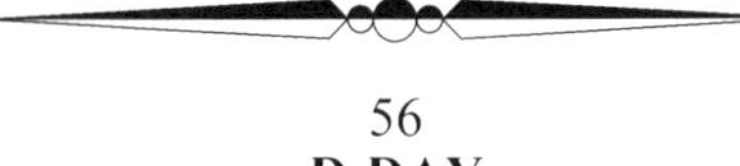

56
D-DAY

As Allied forces were building up in England, American and British planes struck targets in Germany and other areas on the Continent under Nazi control. The cost to the Allies was staggering, with tens of thousands of aircraft lost and the airmen on board killed, but the campaign led to dominance of the skies. By mid-1944, Allied troops were prepared to liberate France and the rest of Europe.

The supreme commander of Allied forces in Europe, U.S. General Dwight D. Eisenhower, ordered the long-awaited assault to begin on the morning of June 6, designated by the military as D-Day. Many Nazi coastal commanders had left their posts and were back in Germany or elsewhere in France because German forecasters expected the stormy weather in the English Channel and along the French coast to continue for several more days. Allied forecasters, on the other hand, had accurately predicted a slight break in the weather, which made an invasion possible.

Adding to the element of surprise was an elaborate deception campaign that convinced Hitler that the Allied invasion would begin at Calais, the closest French town to England, just 20 miles across the Channel. Instead, the offensive, codenamed Operation Overlord, began 200 miles south, in the Normandy region of France. The Allies divided a 50-mile stretch of the coastline into five sectors. Aircraft and warships pounded Nazi coastal batteries before 4,000 landing craft put 133,000 soldiers and their equipment and supplies ashore. It was the largest amphibious invasion in history. More than 23,000 other troops had already begun landing behind the beaches in parachutes and gliders before dawn.

Casualties were heaviest in the sector named Omaha Beach, where German machine guns and artillery cut down U.S. troops. Battle plans went awry as commanders were killed and vital equipment was taken out by enemy fire or sank before reaching shore, but the soldiers did not panic in the chaos and carnage. Lower-level officers and enlisted men stepped up and improvised to establish beachheads. Within hours, the Allies had breached the Atlantic Wall, coastal fortifications years under construction and touted by the Nazis as impregnable.

Twenty-five hundred Americans died on the first day of the Normandy Invasion. That evening, President Roosevelt led the nation in a solemn six-minute prayer broadcast over the radio.

In less than a month, a million troops had landed on French soil. As they advanced and liberated areas held by the Germans, Allied soldiers discovered numerous concentration camps where an untold number of prisoners, mostly civilians, had been tortured and killed by the Nazis. Some prisoners had been subjected to medical experimentation.

In labor concentration camps, many captives forced to work in horrific conditions eventually succumbed to disease or exhaustion. Other prisons were death camps designed to kill quickly, systematically, and en masse, sparing neither children nor the handicapped. Camp guards shot the prisoners or stripped off their clothing and herded them into rooms that were then filled with poison gas. Gold dental fillings removed from the mouths of the dead went into the German treasury. Axis manufacturers used the hair of executed women and girls to make felt and yarn.

The genocide was on such a colossal scale that burying all the victims individually was impossible. The Germans resorted to burning the corpses in large ovens or in open pits. More than a million people were killed at the Auschwitz extermination camp in Poland. Almost as many died at Treblinka, also in Poland. Six million Jews perished in the Holocaust along with 20 million people from other ethnic groups, including Ukrainians, Russians, Poles, and Yugoslavians.

In December of 1944, Hitler launched a last, desperate offensive to stop the Allied advance. At the Battle of the Bulge, U.S. forces suffered approximately 80,000 casualties, making the month-long engagement the bloodiest of the entire war. After beating back the assault, American and British troops raced toward Berlin from the west. The Soviet army, approaching from the east, entered the German capital first. Adolph Hitler committed suicide before the Russians could kill or capture him. When Germany surrendered on May 8, 1945, Allied nations all over the world celebrated V-E Day (Victory-in-Europe).

President Roosevelt did not live to see Germany's defeat. He died a month earlier, after beginning a fourth term in office. He had been president since 1933.* The vice president, Harry S. Truman, succeeded him as brutal fighting continued in the Pacific Theater against the Japanese.

* *The framers of the Constitution did not limit the number of four-year terms a president could serve. George Washington did not seek re-election after his second term, and his successors before FDR followed that precedent. With ratification of the 22nd Amendment in 1951, presidents became constitutionally limited to no more than two elected terms. Members of the U.S. Congress are not subject to term limits, and many become career politicians.*

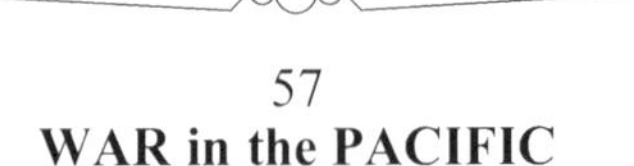

57
WAR in the PACIFIC

After attacking Hawaii on December 7, 1941, the Japanese captured the U.S. territories of Guam and Wake Island and swept across the Pacific and Southeast Asia. In the Philippines, 12,000 U.S. troops and 60,000 Filipino troops surrendered on the Bataan peninsula and were forced to walk 65 miles to a prison camp. The ordeal is remembered as the Bataan Death March because of the atrocities committed by the Japanese. At least 600 Americans and 5,000 Filipinos were killed during the journey. Thousands more would die in captivity. On the Philippine island fortress of Corregidor, 11,000 American and Filipino soldiers held out for another month before they, too, were taken prisoner. The surrender of the Philippines remains the largest capitulation of U.S. forces in history.

Riding this wave of success, the Japanese were shocked to find the U.S. suddenly able to attack their homeland. In April of 1942, 16 B-25 bombers took off from the aircraft carrier USS *Hornet* steaming 650 miles off the coast of Japan. The squadron, commanded by Colonel Jimmy Doolittle, hit targets in six Japanese cities, including the capital, Tokyo. One of the planes then diverted to Russia for reasons never revealed. The rest headed toward airfields controlled by Chinese allies as planned, but they ran out of fuel. The airmen bailed out over other parts of China, crash-landed, or ditched in the ocean close to shore. Chinese soldiers and civilians hid the Americans despite an intense search by the Japanese military that left thousands of Chinese dead. All but seven of the 80 Doolittle Raiders eventually made it to safety. For his valor and leadership "above the call of duty," Doolittle received the Medal of Honor, the highest military decoration awarded by the U.S.

The success of the daring daytime attack, less than five months after Pearl Harbor, was incalculable and extended far beyond the mission itself. It boosted American morale when the outlook was bleak, and it proved that the enemy was not invincible. Moreover, the fear of another such attack caused the Japanese to hold back aircraft to protect their homeland when those planes could have been used against the Allies on the war's front lines. The raid made Japan painfully aware of its blunder in attacking Hawaii when America's carriers were not in port.

The Allies halted Japan's advance across the Pacific in May 1942 at the Battle of the Coral Sea, near New Guinea and Australia. The next major engagement took place at Midway, a tiny American atoll 3,000 miles to the northeast, in the central Pacific. The Japanese were unaware that the United States had cracked their secret code used to encrypt messages.* U.S. commanders knew from intercepted radio transmissions that Japan intended to attack the remote American outpost. The ensuing battle cost the Japanese four aircraft carriers (all had attacked Pearl Harbor), a navy cruiser, 300 aircraft, and 3,000 sailors and pilots, losses from which the Imperial Navy never fully recovered.

The Battle of Midway was a turning point, but the enemy remained formidable throughout most of the Pacific. The U.S. devised a brilliant strategy known as "island hopping" or "leapfrogging," bypassing heavily defended areas to invade more vulnerable ones. It cut supply lines to the Japanese strongholds, leaving them to "wither on the vine," which conserved American resources and sped up the advance toward Japan.

U.S. forces commanded by Admiral Chester Nimitz, General Douglas MacArthur, and Admiral William "Bull" Halsey fought their way across northern New Guinea and from one island chain to another: the Solomons (especially the island of Guadalcanal), the Gilberts (Tarawa), the Marshalls (Kwajalein), the Marianas (Saipan), and the Palaus (Peleliu). American submarines sank 1,300 Japanese warships and merchant vessels. Carriers that could launch a hundred planes helped the U.S. gain air superiority. Ingenious mobile dry docks that could lift any ship out of the water made major repairs possible in far-flung combat zones. Artillery shells with proximity fuses, a technology that only the Allies had, increased the lethality of naval guns and land-based batteries exponentially.

In October 1944 the campaign to retake the Philippines began with the Battle of Leyte Gulf, the largest naval engagement in history. The Japanese navy was defeated so decisively that it ceased to be a significant threat for the remainder of the war. Manila was liberated in March 1945.

As the warfront moved closer to their homeland, desperate Japanese commanders sent thousands of pilots on suicidal *kamikaze* missions to crash their aircraft into U.S. ships. The attacks killed 5,000 sailors, wounded just as many, sank 50 ships and damaged 300 others. Land battles were also extremely costly because Japanese soldiers often kept fighting after they had lost all chance of victory. Six thousand Marines died taking the tiny island of Iwo Jima. The Battle of Okinawa cost the lives of 12,000 American troops.

* *Neither the Japanese nor the Germans were ever able to decipher coded U.S. messages transmitted and received by Native American military personnel in their tribal languages. Most "code talkers" were Navajo.*

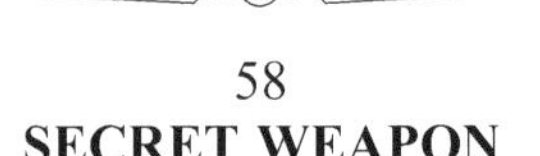

58
SECRET WEAPON

By July 1945, the Allies had advanced across the Pacific to Japan itself. Planes and ships bombarded the country repeatedly, but the Japanese would not lay down their arms. U.S. military planners estimated that an amphibious invasion to end the war could cost millions of lives, counting American troops, Allied prisoners of war being held in Japan, and Japanese troops and civilians.

Since the beginning of hostilities, the U.S. had been working intensely on the Manhattan Project, a top-secret program to develop an instrument of war more powerful and destructive than anything in history: the atom bomb. After the bomb was successfully tested, the United States gave the enemy an ultimatum: surrender unconditionally or face annihilation. When the government of Japan refused to yield, President Truman gave the order to use the new weapon.

On August 6, a U.S. B-29 bomber nicknamed *Enola Gay* took off from Tinian, a recently captured island in the Marianas. After a seven-hour flight to the target, the crew dropped an atom bomb on Hiroshima, a major port and military headquarters in southwestern Japan. The weapon obliterated the city, killing at least 70,000 and seriously injuring tens of thousands.

But the Japanese did not give up. Three days later, the U.S. dropped an atom bomb on Nagasaki, the site of a large steel and armament factory. The explosion, billowing up in a mushroom cloud, destroyed that city as well and proved to be the final blow. Japan surrendered on August 14, 1945, or V-J Day (Victory-over-Japan).*

Spontaneous celebrations erupted around the world when news broke that the war was over. In cities throughout the United States, people gathered in the streets to dance and cheer. Families and friends anxiously awaited the homecoming of the men and women in uniform, but 405,000 American soldiers, sailors, airmen, and marines would not return. The war had cost at least 60 million lives worldwide.

The Allies prosecuted notorious Axis leaders and operatives for the bloodshed, destruction, and suffering they had caused. Tribunals in Nuremberg, Germany, and elsewhere executed hundreds of Nazis and imprisoned many more. A thousand Japanese war criminals were sentenced to death in similar trials in Tokyo and other locations. The Allies allowed Emperor Hirohito to remain as a figurehead, however.

Two months after the war's end, countries across the globe came together to form the United Nations (U.N.) to help keep the peace. In contrast with America's stance toward the League of Nations following World War I, the United States was the principal supporter of this new international organization, headquartered in New York City.

* *The official surrender documents were signed on September 2 in a formal ceremony aboard the battleship USS* Missouri *anchored in Tokyo Bay.*

59
BABY BOOM, MARSHALL PLAN, and ISRAEL

The U.S. birth rate rose sharply following the return of 16 million troops to civilian life after their World War II service. The "baby boom generation" (birthdates roughly 1945-64) would have an immense impact on the economy and on society in general for decades.

Other factors also contributed to the nation's successful shift back to peacetime production:

- The U.S. mainland remained virtually unscathed during the war.*
- There was pent-up demand after a decade of economic depression and four years of wartime rationing.
- Americans had extra money to spend. Jobs had been plentiful during the war, and the savings rate was high.
- Wartime research led to new technologies and new products.
- The G.I. Bill† assisted veterans with the transition back to the private sector. In addition to loans and unemployment compensation, the legislation provided aid for vocational training and college. Consequently, a flood of skilled laborers and professionals entered the workforce.

America's postwar prosperity enabled the U.S. to provide aid to foreign countries. The war left much of Europe in ruins. Millions of people were without basic necessities, and some were near starvation. President Truman's secretary of state, George C. Marshall, developed a recovery plan for Europe, including western Germany. The Marshall Plan was remarkably effective. By the end of 1951, most economies in Western Europe were stronger than before the war.

Though not included in the Marshall Plan, Japan also received enormous help rebuilding its economy and infrastructure. The success there, too, was phenomenal. West Germany and Japan became allies of the United States, but tight restrictions placed on both countries kept them incapable of waging war again.

Nazi atrocities against Jews before and during World War II made much of the world sympathetic to the creation of a Jewish state in Palestine, an area along the eastern Mediterranean Sea that includes the ancient city of Jerusalem. For centuries, the dispersed Jewish people had longed to gather to that Middle East region regarded by them as their homeland from Biblical times. Arab residents were just as convinced that the land was their own ancestral home.

In 1947 the United Nations approved a plan to partition Palestine into two territories, one Jewish and the other Arab. The provisional Jewish government declared independence the following year, and President Truman immediately gave formal U.S. recognition to the new nation of Israel. The first Arab-Israeli war ensued, and hostilities have continued ever since.

* *The Japanese did, however, seize two of the Aleutian Islands in Alaska, and a balloon bomb launched from Japan killed five children and an adult in Oregon. On the East Coast, German U-boats deposited commando units in New York and Florida to destroy infrastructure and industrial targets, but the Nazis were captured and executed before they did any damage. During World War I, a similar group of German saboteurs destroyed a major munitions depot near the Statue of Liberty.*

† *"G.I." was an abbreviation originally used by the U.S. Army for "galvanized iron," the material from which many supplies were made. Later, it stood for "government issue," or any article distributed by the military. Finally, it came to mean any member of the United States armed forces.*

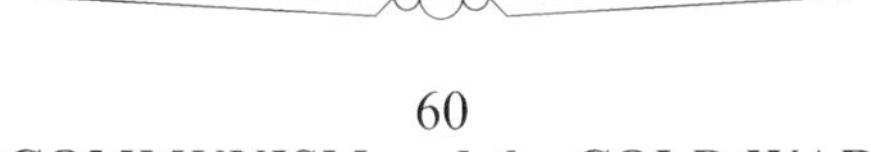

60
COMMUNISM and the COLD WAR

America's principal ally in the Second World War, besides Great Britain, was the U.S.S.R., a communist nation. Under communism, one political party controls the government and regulates much of the activity in a country. Civil liberties are severely limited, including private property ownership.

After the war, the Russians assumed control of the eastern part of Germany, and the other major Allied powers – the U.S., Great Britain, and France – took over the western part. Berlin, located deep inside Soviet-controlled eastern Germany, was similarly divided into an eastern sector held by the Russians and a western sector overseen by the other Allies.

The U.S.S.R. also sought control of Eastern Europe, which included Poland, Czechoslovakia, Hungary, Romania, Bulgaria, and Albania. In those countries, millions of ethnic Germans were expelled, and the Russians set up communist governments that, in one way or another, took orders from the Kremlin, the Soviet headquarters in the capital of Moscow, Russia. Winston Churchill warned in 1946 that an "Iron Curtain" had descended across the continent. The metaphor described the closing off of Eastern Europe from the democratic capitalist countries of Western Europe. A Cold War had begun. Provocative actions by the communists threatened to escalate into a "hot war" (shooting war) with Western nations.

The U.S. adopted a new foreign policy to contain Russia's efforts to expand its communist influence. Under the Truman Doctrine, America extended both economic and military aid to free peoples "resisting attempted subjugation by armed minorities or by outside pressures."

A major crisis in the Cold War arose in 1948 when the communists cut off railway, highway, and waterway access into western Berlin, an enclave of democracy and capitalism surrounded by communist eastern Germany. Avoiding a direct confrontation on the ground, the U.S. and other Western nations thwarted the blockade with a massive airlift of supplies to the isolated western half of the divided city. The Berlin Airlift continued until the communists lifted the blockade the following year.

To counter the threat posed by the U.S.S.R. and its Eastern Bloc partners, the United States and 11 other nations formed a security alliance called the North Atlantic Treaty Organization (NATO).* That same year, 1949, President Truman made the sobering announcement that the Russians had successfully tested an atom bomb. America had remained the world's sole atomic power for only four years. The U.S. and the Soviet Union would go on to build weapons with a thousand times more destructive power than the atom bombs dropped on Japan, and both nations would develop a triad of planes, submarines, and underground missile silos capable of delivering nuclear strikes anywhere on earth.

The nuclear arms race and the spread of communism dominated U.S. foreign policy for decades. In the face of these ongoing threats, and unlike previous postwar periods, the United States maintained a high level of military readiness to ensure national security, support its allies, and protect American interests around the world.† The military worked closely with private companies (defense contractors) to constantly upgrade weapons systems. President Dwight D. Eisenhower warned citizens to keep this "military-industrial complex" from gaining undue political and economic influence.

Nuclear technology was not used strictly for weapons. In 1957 America's first commercial nuclear power plant for generating electricity went into service in western Pennsylvania.

Reports of communist subversives in the U.S. prompted investigations of federal employees and began a period dubbed the Red Scare. The color red had long been associated with communism. Between 1947 and 1956, the government screened five million actual and prospective federal workers and dismissed 2,700 as security risks; 12,000 resigned.

Alger Hiss had held a number of government positions before a U.S. district court found him guilty of perjury in connection with an espionage investigation. The case against Julius and Ethel Rosenberg was more alarming. They were convicted of treason for supplying the Russians with classified information about America's atomic weapons program. The couple was executed in the electric chair in 1953.

The government also investigated the entertainment industry for communist ties. Movie studios blacklisted those who became suspects, damaging or ruining their careers.

Senator Joseph McCarthy of Wisconsin gained national attention by claiming that communists had infiltrated the U.S. government, including the military. His tactics and decorum during congressional hearings in 1954 led to his being formally censured by the Senate.

* *NATO currently has 32 member nations. The newest member, Sweden, joined the alliance in 2024.*

† *Of the 1.3 million American troops on active duty in 2025, 1.2 million were based in the U.S., with 164,000 in California, 123,000 in Virginia, 114,000 in Texas, 96,000 in North Carolina, 46,000 in Hawaii, and 21,000 in Alaska. Among those stationed in approximately 800 U.S. military installations in foreign lands, 53,000 were in Japan, 36,000 in Germany, 24,000 in South Korea, 13,000 in Italy, and 10,000 in Britain. An additional 767,000 troops served in the National Guard and the Reserves.*

Since the Founding, around 50 million Americans have served in the military, and more than a million have lost their lives.

61
CHINA and KOREA

After the Second World War, Chinese communists under the leadership of Mao Tse-tung renewed their civil war to overthrow the non-communist pro-Western Nationalist government in China led by Chiang

Kai-shek. The U.S. did not send troops but otherwise supported the Nationalists. It was not enough. In 1949, Chiang and his defeated followers fled to Taiwan (formerly known as Formosa), an island off the Chinese coast. The victorious Mao declared his People's Republic of China (PRC) the legitimate government. In America, it was more common to refer to mainland China as Red China or Communist China.

In the closing days of World War II, the United States and the Soviet Union agreed to divide the Korean peninsula along the 38th parallel, or latitude line. The U.S. took control of the South and supported the creation of a representative government. Russia took control of the North and installed a communist government.*

In 1950 North Korea invaded the South. Combat troops from the United States and 15 other U.N. countries joined South Koreans in a coalition to defend the country. American General Douglas MacArthur was given command of the multinational forces. The communists almost overran South Korea before the coalition could launch a counter-offensive beginning with an amphibious landing at Inchon.

After regaining control of the South, coalition troops pushed far into North Korea, close to the Chinese border. With U.N. forces poised to win control of the entire peninsula, China sent 300,000 soldiers across the Yalu River into Korea, forcing coalition troops to make a costly fighting retreat back into the South in sub-zero weather. In an epic battle at the Chosin Reservoir, encircled and vastly outnumbered U.S. troops broke through communist lines to avoid annihilation.

General MacArthur advocated a strategy for total victory that included the bombing of China to keep supplies and reinforcements from coming down into Korea. Neither President Truman nor the other political leaders of the coalition supported such a move, which would have risked all-out war with China, Soviet retaliation in Europe, and possibly a nuclear confrontation with the Soviets. The decision was made to maintain a defensive position near the 38th parallel while seeking a negotiated settlement. After MacArthur privately and publicly challenged the president's policy of containment and limited war, Truman replaced him with General Matthew Ridgway.

Negotiations to end the fighting began in 1951. A truce signed two years later left Korea divided roughly as it had been before, but the war never officially ended, and relations between the two Koreas remained antagonistic. Thirty-seven thousand American servicemen died in the conflict, and 103,000 were wounded.

* *The Soviets appointed Kim Il-sung as the head of North Korea in 1948. After he died in 1994, his son, Kim Jong-il, took over. In 2011, the communist dynasty continued when Kim Jong-un assumed power following the death of his father.*

62
CIVIL RIGHTS, TELEVISION, INTERSTATES, and ROCK & ROLL

In the aftermath of America's Civil War, state and local governments, primarily in the South, passed measures to keep blacks and whites apart. In 1896, the U.S. Supreme Court ruled in *Plessy v. Ferguson* that separate accommodations for black passengers on Louisiana trains did not deprive them of equal protection under the law, as guaranteed by the 14th Amendment to the Constitution. Segregation also manifested itself in ways not specifically addressed by law. This legal and cultural separation of the races was known as "Jim Crow."

From the Revolutionary War to World War II and afterward, it was common for blacks in the U.S. military to serve in segregated units.* In 1948 President Truman issued an executive order to begin the integration of the armed services, a goal that was achieved during the Korean War.

Before the 1950s, separate schools for black and white children were prevalent in the United States. That began to change when Oliver Brown and other African-American parents in Topeka, Kansas, filed a federal lawsuit against the local school board over its policy of racial segregation. The plaintiffs contended that their children were being denied an equal education because black schools were inferior.

The district court sided with the school board, but the decision was appealed. In *Brown v. Board of Education*, the Supreme Court in 1954 reversed the lower court's ruling and found in favor of the plaintiffs, striking down the "separate but equal" doctrine in public education as a violation of the 14th Amendment. By breaking from precedent and repudiating the *Plessy* decision, the high court paved the way for the integration of black and white children in all public schools.

In 1957, only 20 percent of blacks in the U.S. were registered to vote. President Eisenhower signed a civil rights bill that year to strengthen African-American voting rights, which had been suppressed for decades in parts of the South through poll taxes, literacy tests, and intimidation.†

A new form of mass communication rose to prominence in the Fifties. An Idaho farm boy, Philo T. Farnsworth, conceived the basic elements of the technology back in the 1920s. Television was ready for market when World War II broke out, but wartime restrictions on nonmilitary manufacturing forced a delay. After the war, television grew into a major industry. The first TV sets had small screens, the picture was in black and white, and programming was very limited, but by 1955, two-thirds of American households owned a TV.

Civilian air travel benefited from the technological advances made in military aviation during World War II. Passenger planes after the war flew farther, faster, and higher. Electronic equipment helped pilots avoid dangerous weather. Airplanes replaced trains and ocean liners as the preferred mode of mass transportation over long distances. In 1958 the first American jet airliner, the Boeing 707, went into service.

An ambitious plan championed by President Eisenhower to construct an interstate road system got underway in the 1950s. These multi-lane divided highways, free of stop signs and traffic lights, made it possible to travel from Florida to Michigan on just one road, Interstate 75 (I-75). Interstate 80 stretched all the way from New Jersey to California. The 47,000 miles of interstate highways changed the face of America and have had a profound impact on the economy.

In music, the Big Bands of the 1930s and '40s gave way to a new genre called rock and roll. Fans hailed Elvis Presley as the "King" of the new music. The main instruments used – guitar, bass, keyboard, and drums – enabled singers to provide their own accompaniment.

After many decades as U.S. territories, Alaska and Hawaii were admitted as the 49th and 50th states in 1959. With statehood came representation in Congress and the right of citizens to vote in congressional and presidential elections. For the first time since 1912, when New Mexico and Arizona achieved statehood, stars had to be added to the American flag to reflect the current number of states. Alaska and Hawaii are the only non-contiguous states.

* *The Tuskegee Airmen, a segregated unit of African-American fighter pilots, served with distinction in Europe during World War II. From 1796 to 1942, the Marine Corps barred blacks from their ranks.*

† *The 24th Amendment banned poll taxes constitutionally in 1964. According to U.S. Census Bureau estimates, in 2024, 70% of black citizens were registered to vote, and 85% voted; 75% of white citizens were registered, and 90% voted. Between 48 million and 82 million eligible voters did not vote.*

63
SPUTNIK, CASTRO, and KENNEDY

In 1957, Russia shocked the world, especially the U.S., by launching the first satellite into space. Satellites are unmanned spacecraft used for gathering scientific data and for communications, military surveillance, and weather forecasting. The Soviets called their satellite *Sputnik*. Its orbital path took it over the United States. The U.S. put its first satellite into orbit the following year. Along with the arms race, America and the U.S.S.R. were now also competitors in a space race.

Relations between the two superpowers were strained further when the Soviets shot down an American U-2 spy plane flying high over Russia. The pilot bailed out and was captured. After first claiming that the aircraft had been conducting weather research, the Eisenhower administration acknowledged that its mission was part of the extensive aerial reconnaissance conducted covertly by the United States to guard against a surprise attack like Pearl Harbor.

Communism spread in the Western Hemisphere in the 1950s. The most alarming instance was in Cuba. When Fidel Castro overthrew the dictator of that island in 1959, most Americans initially viewed it as a positive development, but Castro turned out to be a communist who confiscated private property and ruled as a dictator himself. The United States imposed an economic embargo against Cuba and severed diplomatic relations when that island nation, only 90 miles off the southern coast of Florida, aligned itself with the Soviet Union.

In the presidential election of 1960, Richard Nixon, vice president in the Eisenhower administration, was the Republican nominee, and John F. Kennedy, the junior senator from Massachusetts, was the Democratic nominee. The candidates began a campaign tradition of debating each other on live television. Kennedy's victory on Election Day made him, at age 43, the youngest president ever elected.*

* *Teddy Roosevelt became president at age 42 upon William McKinley's death, but he had been elected as vice president.*

64
SUPERPOWER STANDOFF

Soon after his inauguration, President Kennedy signed an executive order creating the Peace Corps, a federal agency that recruits American volunteers to work for two years improving the lives of people around the world. Members provide assistance in agriculture, health, youth development, education, economic development, and the environment.*

In April of 1961, the president authorized an invasion of Cuba to overthrow the communist dictatorship of Fidel Castro with help from opposition groups on the island. The U.S. Central Intelligence Agency (CIA), which orchestrated the plan, hoped to obscure American involvement by recruiting 1,500 Cuban exiles living in Miami, Florida, to carry out the operation. Support planes painted in the colors of the Cuban air force added to the deception.

The amphibious landing took place on the southern coast of Cuba at the Bay of Pigs. Kennedy canceled vital air support after the assault was already underway. The mission failed after three days. Of the CIA operatives involved in the action, 100 were killed and 1,200 were taken prisoner.† The Castro regime executed hundreds of dissident Cuban citizens in the subsequent crackdown.

In Europe, so many East Germans were fleeing their stark and oppressive conditions that it was having a serious negative effect on that communist country's economy and political standing in the world. To stem the flow of escapees, the East German government, with support from the Soviet Union, began constructing a wall around democratic West Berlin in August of 1961. This heightened tensions because it was not known if the communists intended to block access to the city, as they had done in 1948-49. But there was a bigger concern. If the real objective was a communist takeover, the United States might have had to use its tactical (battlefield) nuclear weapons to defend the city.

Kennedy dispatched his vice president to West Berlin. In a show of strength, he also sent 1,500 American soldiers to reinforce the military units already there from the United States and other Allied nations. After traveling in a large convoy over one of the established highway access routes through East Germany, the troops were allowed to pass through communist checkpoints and enter West Berlin. The city remained free and its access to the outside world remained open, but the communists continued building the wall, and they severed rail lines at the city's border to keep East Germans from escaping to freedom in West Berlin. The Berlin Wall would stand as a symbol of the Cold War for decades.

A more serious threat arose in 1962. Photographs taken by U.S. satellites and spy planes revealed the existence of Soviet missiles in Cuba that could be armed with nuclear warheads and hit American cities within minutes. The president considered using air strikes or a full military invasion to destroy the missile sites, but he opted for a blockade of Cuba using the Navy, the Coast Guard, and the Air Force to prevent the Soviets from supplying any more offensive weapons.

Not knowing how the Russians would respond, America prepared for nuclear war with its Cold War adversary. By this time, the United States and the U.S.S.R. possessed enough weapons to destroy the major cities of both countries in a full-scale nuclear exchange, a scenario that has been called "mutually assured destruction." After several tense days, the Soviets agreed to dismantle their missile installations in Cuba in return for a U.S. pledge to remove its missiles from Turkey, a country bordering the Soviet Union.

* *The Peace Corps has sent 240,000 volunteers to 144 countries since its inception.*

† *In 1962, Castro released the captured Cuban exiles to the United States in exchange for $3 million in cash and $53 million worth of medical supplies and other goods raised from private donations.*

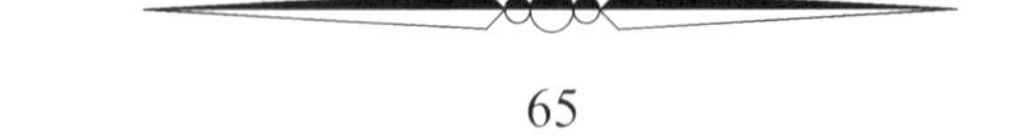

65
ASSASSINATION and the GREAT SOCIETY

On November 22, 1963, President Kennedy was in Texas for a second day to shore up support for his re-election. As he and the first lady rode through downtown Dallas waving to crowds from an open limousine, he was shot by an unseen gunman. The Secret Service, responsible for protecting the president, rushed him to a hospital, where doctors pronounced him dead.* Local police arrested Lee Harvey Oswald for the shooting an hour later.

Vice President Lyndon Johnson, who had been riding in the motorcade two cars behind Kennedy, was sworn in as president aboard Air Force One that afternoon at the Dallas airport. With the slain president's distraught widow standing beside her husband's successor, the oath of office was administered by a local federal judge, a woman appointed by Kennedy. After the solemn ceremony, the presidential plane took off for the return flight to Washington, D.C., carrying Kennedy's casket.

Two days later, authorities were transferring Oswald to a different Dallas jail when a man stepped out from a crowd of onlookers and fatally shot him. Police quickly subdued and arrested the assailant.

Johnson won the 1964 presidential election in a landslide. He pushed through legislation that provided extensive and sustained federal funding to wage a "War on Poverty" and bring about a "Great Society" in America.

The Head Start program helped disadvantaged children of preschool age, and lawmakers appropriated money for education at the elementary, secondary, and college levels. Funds were also made available for job training and loans to small businesses. The government created the National Endowment for the Arts, the National Endowment for the Humanities, the Corporation for Public Broadcasting, and two new cabinet-level agencies: the Department of Housing & Urban Development (HUD) and the Department of Transportation (DOT).

Medicare subsidized the health care of Americans 65 and older. Medicaid did the same for needy families and low-income individuals under 65.† The poor also became eligible for food stamps (later a government debit card) to purchase groceries.[‡] With these programs and others, the number of citizens receiving direct financial assistance from the government rose considerably.

In 1965 a new immigration law abolished the national origins formula created in the 1920s and gave foreigners of every nationality an equal opportunity to become U.S. citizens. The legislation also marked the first time that reuniting families, what has been called "chain migration," was given priority over the job skills of applicants. Annual ceilings were set for each hemisphere – 170,000 for the Eastern and 120,000 for the Western – but foreigners with immediate family members who were already American citizens or permanent resident aliens were not subject to the ceilings. As a result, the number of immigrant visas issued far exceeded the stated limits.[§]

* *Assassins killed two other presidents besides Kennedy and Lincoln: James Garfield in 1881 and William McKinley in 1901.*

† *Medicare and Medicaid together account for 24% of the current federal budget. For perspective, defense spending is 13%.*

‡ *Food stamp statistics from the U.S. Department of Agriculture:*

	Recipients	*Households*	*% of Pop*	*Expenditures*
2000	*17M*	*7M*	*6%*	*$15B*
2015	*46M*	*23M*	*14%*	*$70B*
2019	*36M*	*18M*	*11%*	*$56B*
2024	*42M*	*22M*	*12%*	*$94B*

§ *In 2023, more than a million immigrants became legal permanent U.S. residents. Since 1960, the main countries of origin of the foreign-born U.S. population have shifted from Europe to Latin America and Asia. According to the Census Bureau:*

Foreign-born Population

	1960	*2023*
in millions	*10*	*49*
% tot pop	*5%*	*15%*
% citizens	*71%**	*51%*

** average of 1950 & 1970*

Pop Speaking Foreign Lang at Home

1980 – 11% *2023 – 22%*

Foreign-born Population by Region of Origin

	1960	*2023*
Europe	*75%*	*10%*
Canada	*10%*	*1%*
Latin America	*9%*	*53%*
Asia	*5%*	*30%*
Africa	*0%*	*5%*
Other	*1%*	*1%*

66
I HAVE A DREAM

In the summer of 1963, Dr. Martin Luther King Jr., leader of the civil rights movement and also a minister, led 250,000 people in a march on Washington, D.C. The event culminated with his visionary speech from the steps of the Lincoln Memorial. He told the crowd:

> I have a dream that one day this nation will rise up and live out the true meaning of its creed: We hold these truths to be self-evident, that all men are created equal. I have a dream that my four little children will one day live in a nation where they will not be judged by the color of their skin but by the content of their character.

Before 1964 it was common in the South to find hotels, restaurants, theaters, restrooms, drinking fountains, and swimming pools designated "whites only." Where admittance was open to all, blacks were often relegated to certain areas such as the balcony of the theater or the back of the bus. A civil rights bill enacted that year outlawed discrimination in public places, employment, and public schools based on race, color, religion, sex, or national origin.

In America's metropolitan areas, a demographic shift that began in the 1940s continued into the '60s as large numbers of families moved to the suburbs, leaving inner cities with predominantly minority populations and a diminished tax base. To achieve racial integration in public schools, some school districts would later implement mandatory busing of students to schools outside the neighborhoods where they lived.

Racial tensions sparked 750 riots between 1964 and 1971. Six days of rioting in the Los Angeles neighborhood of Watts left 34 people dead, a thousand injured, and 800 buildings damaged or destroyed. In Detroit, the Michigan National Guard and the U.S. Army were deployed to restore order during riots in which 43 people died and 2,000 buildings were burned. The most riots occurred in 1968, the year Martin Luther King was assassinated in Memphis, Tennessee.

Amid the unrest, a milestone was reached when Thurgood Marshall, previously chief counsel for the National Association for the Advancement of Colored People (NAACP), became the first African-American appointed to the U.S. Supreme Court.

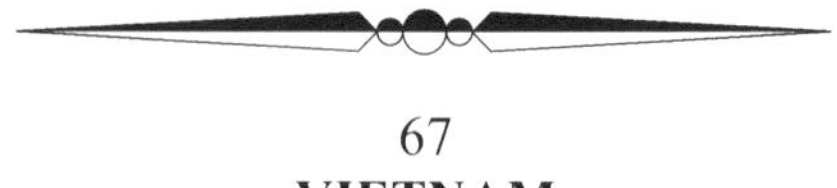

67
VIETNAM

After Vietnamese communists defeated French colonial forces in 1954, diplomats from the U.S., Russia, Britain, France, China, and Indochina partitioned Vietnam much like Korea, with a demarcation line separating the communist North from the pro-Western non-communist South. The U.S. supported South Vietnam with military advisors and weapons because President Eisenhower believed a communist takeover there would have a domino effect and lead to other countries in the region falling to communism. President Kennedy increased U.S. troop levels in Vietnam to 16,000 in 1963.

The following year, three North Vietnamese torpedo boats fired on an American destroyer conducting reconnaissance in disputed international waters in the Gulf of Tonkin. The destroyer returned fire and called in air support. All three North Vietnamese vessels sustained damage but returned to their base. The U.S. ship and its support aircraft were unscathed. This minor naval engagement and an erroneous report of a second attack two days later were the incidents that precipitated a massive and protracted commitment of U.S. armed forces.

President Johnson ordered retaliatory air strikes against North Vietnam. Without declaring war, Congress authorized the president to conduct military operations in Southeast Asia.* Johnson drastically increased troop strength in the region to 500,000 by 1968 as America assumed the primary role in South Vietnam's defense. To disrupt the enemy's supply lines, the U.S. carried out covert operations in Laos and Cambodia, including enormous bombing campaigns. North Vietnam received support from its communist allies, China and Russia.

Televised news reports showing the bloodshed and destruction in Vietnam eroded public support for the war and President Johnson. He decided not to run for re-election, an unusual move for an incumbent.

In 1968 former vice president Richard Nixon launched a second presidential campaign, and this time he won. After taking office, he began withdrawing troops from Vietnam, and South Vietnam's forces took on an ever-increasing role in the war, a process called Vietnamization. Bombing by U.S. aircraft intensified, however, and American and South Vietnamese troops launched attacks on communist sanctuaries in Cambodia.

Opposition to the war continued. The Beatles, Bob Dylan, and other popular artists protested through their music. Demonstrations sprang up across the United States, particularly on college campuses. At Kent State University in Ohio, National Guard troops trying to control a crowd shot and killed four students.

Hundreds of thousands of young men evaded the draft; 90,000 moved to Canada. In 1971, ratification of the 26th Amendment to the Constitution guaranteed voting rights to male and female citizens as young as 18, the age when young men became eligible for the draft. The following year, the U.S. discontinued conscription and made military service voluntary.†

The United States and South Vietnam signed peace accords with North Vietnam in 1973, and America withdrew the last of its troops. What President Nixon called "peace with honor" was a stalemate shakier than the one in Korea. Just two years later, the North Vietnamese conquered the South and united both Vietnams under communist rule. Cambodia and Laos also fell to the communists.

More than three million U.S. troops served in Southeast Asia over the course of the war, and 58,000 sacrificed their lives; 300,000 were wounded. Unlike their counterparts in previous wars, those who made it back home did not return to public celebrations in their honor, and some even faced ridicule for having served.

* *The U.S. Congress has declared war only five times: the War of 1812, the Mexican War, the Spanish-American War, World War I, and World War II.*

† *Nearly all male citizens ages 18 through 25 are still required to register with Selective Service, the federal agency that administers the draft when it is in effect. American women have never been subject to conscription, but more than two million have voluntarily enlisted in the military over the years. The 237,000 women in uniform in 2025 represented 18% of total active-duty personnel.*

68
FEMINISM, DRUGS, and the ENVIRONMENT

Race relations and Vietnam were not the only issues fueling the political and social upheaval of the 1960s; feminism was another. That movement addressed the role of women in society and pushed for an end to sex discrimination. Employment was a chief concern. Women objected to being paid less than men for doing the same work. They sought equal opportunity for jobs deemed suitable only for men, and they wanted to remove the "glass ceiling" that kept women from attaining the top positions in organizations.

The abuse of legal drugs increased in the '60s, as did the use of illegal substances such as marijuana, cocaine, and the hallucinogen LSD. Cohabitation and sexual relations between unmarried individuals began to lose much of the stigma that had existed previously. Abortion became a central issue after a 1973 Supreme Court decision, *Roe v. Wade*, made the procedure legal throughout the country.*

The environment rose in prominence as a political issue. Studies revealed alarming levels of pollution in the air, water, and soil. Environmentalists raised concerns over the destruction of forests and wetlands and the possible extinction of certain species, including the Bald Eagle, a national symbol. President Nixon signed legislation to punish polluters and protect the environment and endangered wildlife. Public and private efforts to recycle newspapers, metal, glass, and plastic gained momentum.

* *In 2022 the high court overturned* Roe v. Wade, *rejecting abortion as a constitutional right and sending questions regarding its legality back to each state.*

Berlin airlift

U.S. troops retreat across the Chosin Reservoir

Television in the 1950s

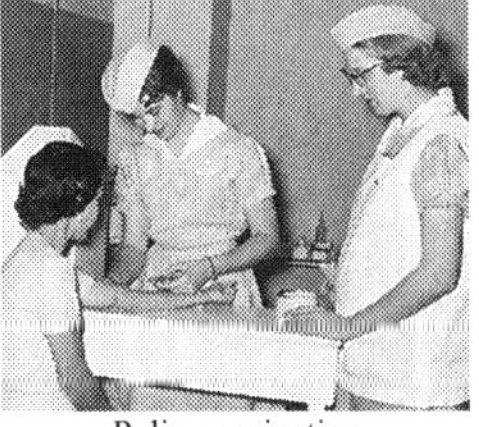
Polio vaccination

Elvis Presley

First U.S. nuclear power station

U.S. military confronts Russian ship during Cuban missile crisis

Nuclear submarine

Underground nuclear missile silo

Dr. Martin Luther King Jr.

President Kennedy (in rear seat) just prior to assassination

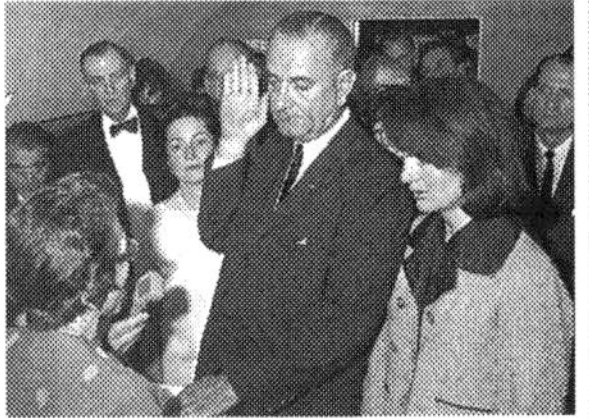
Lyndon Johnson sworn in as president aboard Air Force One

Food Stamp / EBT cards

Vietnam War

Thurgood Marshall

Soldiers deployed in Washington, D.C. after riots

College protests

Drugs

Woodstock Music Festival

Buzz Aldrin salutes flag on the moon

Endangered manatee

Abortion lawsuits

President Nixon (right) resigns

South Vietnamese flee communist takeover

President Carter brokers peace between Israel and Egypt

Iranians storm U.S. embassy

President Reagan at the Berlin Wall in 1987

Sandra Day O'Connor

Personal computers

Gulf War

9/11 terrorist attacks

War in Iraq

President Barack Obama

Situation Room – bin Laden raid

President Donald Trump

Southern border wall

Masking during pandemic

Outdoor ballot drop box

Afghans try to board evacuation aircraft

69
ONE GIANT LEAP FOR MANKIND

The Soviet Union was the early leader in space exploration. The first satellite and the first manned rocket to orbit the earth were Russian. The first American in space was astronaut Alan Shepard, who blasted off from Cape Canaveral, Florida, in 1961 and reached an altitude of 116 miles above the earth before the spacecraft descended by parachute 300 miles downrange in the Atlantic. The 15-minute suborbital flight was a minor achievement compared to what the Soviets had done, but just three weeks later, President Kennedy laid out his vision for America's fledgling space program and set a goal to land a man on the moon and return him safely before the end of the decade. The National Aeronautics and Space Administration (NASA) accepted the bold challenge.

The first American in orbit was John Glenn, who circled the earth three times during a five-hour flight in 1962.* Subsequent flights by other astronauts included many orbits over several days. In addition to manned space missions, the United States launched numerous satellites into orbit and sent probes to explore the solar system.

On July 20, 1969, Neil Armstrong and Buzz Aldrin landed their Apollo 11 spacecraft on the moon. People all over the world watched on live television as Armstrong stepped down onto the powdery lunar surface and said, "That's one small step for [a] man, one giant leap for mankind." The astronauts transmitted back spectacular pictures of the blue Earth suspended in the blackness of space. NASA successfully completed five more manned lunar missions over the next three years.

* *Astronaut Sally Ride was the first American woman in space, making 97 orbits as a crew member aboard the space shuttle in 1983.*

70
CHINA and RUSSIA, WATERGATE, and OIL

Richard Nixon had built a reputation as a staunch anti-communist over many years in elective office. So it came as a surprise when, in his first term as president, he reached out to America's two biggest rivals, both communist nations. Nixon reversed two decades of U.S. foreign policy by officially recognizing the People's Republic of China and supporting its admission to the U.N. In 1972 he became the first president to visit China. Later that year he visited Moscow, another first for a U.S. president. While there, Nixon and the Soviet leader signed an agreement placing limits on the nuclear arsenals of both superpowers.

On the heels of these momentous events, President Nixon's re-election was widely expected. Nevertheless, members of his administration and campaign committee hired operatives to break into the headquarters of the Democratic Party to photograph documents and plant electronic eavesdropping devices. The offices were in the Watergate building in Washington, D.C. Police caught the burglars in the act. The president denied any involvement and easily won re-election, carrying every state but Massachusetts.

In October 1973, war broke out in the Middle East. To regain territory lost in a previous conflict, Egypt and Syria unleashed surprise attacks on Israel during Yom Kippur, the holiest day of the year for Jews. After two days of setbacks, the Israeli military rallied and stopped the Arab advance, but with supplies running low, Israel appealed for help. In the face of Arab and Soviet threats against any nation that came to Israel's aid, President Nixon ordered a massive airlift of military equipment and supplies. The Israelis went on the offensive, took back territory lost in the initial stages, and had the Egyptian army trapped when a negotiated ceasefire went into effect.

The Organization of Petroleum Exporting Countries (OPEC), composed largely of Arab nations, retaliated by imposing an oil embargo against the U.S. The spike in fuel prices contributed to an economic slump in America. The energy crisis resulted in long lines at gas stations and an emphasis on conservation and domestic oil exploration.

Nixon signed legislation authorizing the construction of an 800-mile pipeline in Alaska to carry crude oil from the vast oil field at Prudhoe Bay in the north to the Port of Valdez in the south. From there, the raw material could be transferred to tanker ships and transported to refineries in the lower 48 states. To promote fuel conservation, the federal government mandated a maximum speed limit of 55 miles per hour for the nation's highways.

71
RESIGNATION and HOSTAGES

From the beginning of President Nixon's second term, mounting evidence suggested that, contrary to White House assertions, members of the administration, the president's re-election committee, and Nixon himself were involved in the Watergate affair. During congressional hearings to investigate the matter, a White House aide revealed that the president had made audio recordings of Oval Office meetings. Congress subpoenaed the tapes, which provided evidence that Nixon had abused his authority. While he had not ordered the break-in, he did try to cover up the involvement of others after the fact, which is a crime.

In 1974, with the House of Representatives about to begin impeachment proceedings, Nixon resigned. He is the only president in history to do so. The vice president, Gerald Ford, was sworn in as president immediately following Nixon's departure from the White House.*

President Ford believed it was not in the country's best interest for a former president to be pursued in the courts. Exercising his constitutional prerogative, he granted Nixon a "full, free, and absolute pardon" for any crimes he committed while in office. Other members of Nixon's administration and campaign organization were tried, convicted, and sent to prison.

Jimmy Carter, who had been governor of Georgia, defeated Ford in the 1976 presidential election. President Carter brought the leaders of Egypt and Israel together to negotiate an historic peace accord. It was a remarkable achievement given the fact that the two countries had gone to war with each other five times over the previous 28 years, but two foreign policy setbacks in 1979 overshadowed that success.

The first incident occurred when Iranians stormed the U.S. embassy in the capital city of Tehran and took 52 Americans hostage. Negotiations failed to win their release, and the United States military had to abort a nighttime rescue attempt because of equipment malfunctions in the Iranian desert. The second major challenge came when the Soviet Union invaded Afghanistan.

Domestic problems in the U.S., particularly with the economy, compounded Carter's difficulties. Inflation more than doubled while he was in office. Inflation is a rise in the price of goods and services relative to the money supply. Money decreases in value.

High interest rates were another impediment to economic growth. Most individuals and families borrow money to purchase houses, cars, and other high-dollar items. Businesses take out loans to buy inventory and equipment. A high rate of interest made borrowing more difficult and costly. With money harder to come by, consumers and businesses did not buy as much, and the economy suffered.

In the presidential election of 1980, President Carter lost in a landslide to Ronald Reagan, the former governor of California and a former movie and TV actor. Within minutes after Reagan's swearing-in on January 20, Iran released all the American hostages it had held for 444 days.

* *Gerald R. Ford is the only person to serve as vice president and president without being elected to either office. After Nixon's first vice president resigned in 1973, Ford was appointed vice president in accordance with the 25th Amendment. That amendment also lays out procedures to follow if a president becomes unable to discharge the duties of the office.*

72
REAGAN REVOLUTION

Two months after taking office in 1981, President Reagan narrowly survived an assassination attempt; the bullet stopped less than an inch from his heart. After making a full recovery, he appointed the first female justice to the Supreme Court, Sandra Day O'Connor, one of 402 judicial appointments he would make, more than any other president.

A central theme of Reagan's political philosophy was expressed in his simple statement, "Government is too big, and it spends too much." His plan called for cuts in federal programs and regulations, fewer government employees, and major changes to the tax code that included increased incentives for business investment and dramatically lower income tax rates.*

His policies helped bring down inflation and interest rates and set the stage for nearly eight years of sustained economic growth. Federal revenue increased, but federal spending increased even more, and the national debt rose significantly.† Deficit spending is made possible by government borrowing. The loans are in the form of Treasury bills and other securities issued by the U.S. government that are bought by state and local governments, foreign governments, and individual and corporate investors in America and abroad.‡ The purchases obligate the United States to repay the money plus interest whenever the securities mature, be it short term or long term. The federal government also borrows money from its own accounts, such as the Social Security trust fund.

Part of the rise in government borrowing was due to increased military spending because Reagan regarded the Soviet Union as an "evil empire" bent on world domination. His approach to communist expansion was a departure from the containment policies of previous presidents. He sought to roll back gains the communists had already made. The new strategy was implemented in Eastern Europe, Africa, Cambodia, Afghanistan, and Latin America. Democrats opposed to the policy got legislation passed that prohibited funding of Contra rebels trying to overthrow the communist Sandinista government in Nicaragua.

President Reagan easily won re-election, carrying every state but Minnesota. During his second term, certain members of the administration ignored the Contra funding ban and sent aid using profits from the covert sale of arms to Iran. Some of those involved were tried and convicted, but the president was not found to have broken any laws or to have acted outside his constitutional authority.

In addressing immigration, Reagan signed legislation making it unlawful for companies to hire workers living in the United States illegally, but it also made amnesty available to around three million such individuals who had entered the country before 1982.

Increases in U.S. military spending, the deployment of nuclear missiles in Europe, and the president's insistence on pursuing the Strategic Defense Initiative (SDI) pressured Russia to negotiate a new arms control agreement. The goal of SDI was to build a virtual shield against nuclear missile attacks using ground-based and space-based sensors and interceptors. Although the program was only in the planning stage, SDI played a key role in bringing the two nations together for the first time to reduce, not just limit, their respective nuclear arsenals. In a landmark treaty signed in 1987, Reagan and the new Soviet leader, Mikhail Gorbachev, agreed to eliminate 2,600 nuclear weapons, including an entire category: intermediate-range missiles.

After two terms as vice president in the Reagan administration, George H.W. Bush was elected president in 1988. During his presidency, communist rule in Eastern Europe and the Soviet Union collapsed. Ever since World War II, the U.S.S.R. had dominated Eastern Europe. Then, beginning in 1989, popular uprisings led to free elections. First in Poland, then in Czechoslovakia, Hungary, Bulgaria, and Romania, the control of the communist party came to an end. Unlike his predecessors in the Kremlin, Gorbachev did not try to crush the revolts.

In Germany, citizens began tearing down the Berlin Wall, a symbol of the Cold War since 1961. In 1990, East and West Berlin became one city again, and East Germany and West Germany merged to form a reunified and democratic country after 45 years of division.

Finally, the Soviet Union broke apart. Founded in 1922, it was a nation of republics under the control of the communist party and the Soviet leadership in Moscow. Following the lead of Eastern Europe, the republics rejected communism and, one by one, declared independence. By the end of 1991, the U.S.S.R. no longer existed. In its place were 15 sovereign non-communist countries.

The Cold War – that struggle between East and West, between Soviet-backed communism and democracy and free enterprise, which had kept the world under the specter of nuclear war for decades – was over.

* *Under President Reagan, the top marginal income tax rate for individuals went from 70% to 28%. The highest corporate rate dropped from 46% to 39%.*

† *The national debt grew from $908 billion in 1980 to $2.6 trillion in 1988. By 2025, decades of deficit spending had driven up the debt past $38 trillion, far more than the gross domestic product (GDP), the value of the nation's total annual output of goods and services. Broken down by population, that comes to $112,000 owed by every man, woman, and child in America. Interest on the debt takes up 14% of the current federal budget and costs U.S. taxpayers close to $1 trillion a year.*

‡ *As of 2025, the U.S. government owes investors in Japan $1.2 trillion, the U.K. $865 billion, China $701 billion, Canada $476 billion, Belgium $467 billion, the Cayman Islands $427 billion, and Luxembourg $421 billion.*

73
GULF WAR, CLINTON, and the DIGITAL AGE

Iraq's invasion of Kuwait in 1990 threw the Middle East into crisis and threatened to disrupt the flow of oil through the Persian Gulf, a vital trade route for the world economy. The U.S. assembled a coalition of more than 30 nations to expel the Iraqis. The Gulf War began in January 1991 with an immense air campaign. Ground troops took just four days to liberate Kuwait and force Iraq's capitulation.

After the war, the U.S. economy went into recession. While a recession is less severe than a depression, two million Americans lost their jobs as companies cut costs. President Bush's popularity quickly evaporated in the wake of bad economic news. He lost the 1992 presidential election to Arkansas Governor Bill Clinton.

The economy renewed its expansion. Imports and exports increased after multilateral agreements lowered trade barriers. Interest rates and oil prices remained low. The collapse of the Soviet Union led to reductions in U.S. military spending (the so-called "peace dividend"), and Congress imposed tighter restrictions on other federal spending. The stock market rallied as more Americans than ever before acquired a stake in financial markets through personal investment accounts and 401(k) employee retirement plans.

Investors poured billions of dollars into computer-related companies. The internet was heralded as the basis for a new economy and the centerpiece of a new period in human progress: the Information Age. The period was also dubbed the Digital Age as microchips and computers found their way into practically every business and home. Two companies, Apple and Microsoft, were key players in the proliferation of personal computers.

During President Clinton's second term, the Supreme Court ruled that he could be sued for an incident that allegedly occurred prior to his presidency. The House of Representatives impeached him for perjury and obstruction of justice in connection with the sexual harassment case, but the Senate found him not guilty. He served out the remainder of his term and settled the civil lawsuit out of court.

74
ELECTIONS and ELECTORS

The Constitution requires states to hold federal elections every two years. More specific timing was left up to the legislative branch. In 1792, Congress designated the month of November in even years but gave each state the flexibility of conducting the election on any day in that month. November came after the fall harvest and before winter storms impeded travel over unimproved roads.

With the advent of the telegraph, election results in one state could be quickly communicated and possibly influence voting in other states later in the month. So in 1845, Congress mandated a single federal Election Day throughout the country: the first Tuesday after the first Monday in November. Elections for state and local offices are usually held at the same time.

Nearly all citizens 18 and older may have a voice in elections. In most states, when people register to vote in the county where they reside, they declare themselves as a Republican or a Democrat, or a person may register as an independent, unaffiliated with either party. Political parties have different goals for America and different ideas about the size and role of government. Elections are contests between political parties as well as candidates. Party candidates who win the presidency or a majority of congressional seats give their party more power to enact its platform.

Party members who seek elective office at the local, state, or federal level must first win their party's nomination by defeating fellow party candidates vying for the same governmental office. These intra-party battles are fought in preliminary elections, or primaries, sponsored separately by the Democratic Party and the Republican Party.

Voter eligibility in the primaries varies. If a particular local or state primary is closed, the sponsoring party allows only its members to vote. In a semi-closed primary, independent voters may also participate. In an open primary, party members and independents and members of the opposing party are all allowed to cast ballots. In the primaries as well as on Election Day in November, the general election, citizens vote in person at their assigned local precinct polling stations, or they cast their ballots by mail.*

To become a party's nominee for a seat in the House of Representatives, a candidate has to win the primary in his or her own congressional district. A candidate for the U.S. Senate must win a statewide primary. To clinch a party's presidential nomination, a candidate must compete in primaries or caucuses (a less formal method of voting) in all the states.† The presidential candidate who receives the most votes in these state contests usually becomes the party's nominee. The official nomination takes place at the party's national convention held the summer before the general election. Delegates from every state attend. Before or during the convention, the presumptive presidential nominee chooses a running mate, or nominee for vice president, to complete the ticket.

On Election Day in November, all registered voters may cast a ballot for either the Republican nominee, the Democrat nominee, or the occasional independent candidate to determine who will occupy each contested office for the next term. Those newly elected or re-elected as president, senator, or representative take their oaths of office‡ and begin serving the following January to allow time for a smooth transition with outgoing office holders. Since ratification of the 20th Amendment in 1933, members of Congress are sworn in on January 3 or thereabouts, and the inauguration of the president takes place on January 20.

The presidential election in the year 2000 was one of the most controversial in history and renewed debate about the process. As stipulated by Article II of the Constitution, the president is not chosen directly by the votes of the people (the popular vote) but by electors.[§]

The number of electors allotted to a state is equal to the size of that state's delegation in the U.S. Congress, i.e., two senators plus however many members the state has in the House of Representatives. Hence, a state with 10 House districts is allotted 12 electors. The number of electors in the entire country is equal to the total number of seats in the House (435), plus the total number of Senate seats (100), plus three electors from the capital city, Washington, D.C. The total 538 electors, chosen anew at the state level with each presidential election, are known collectively as the Electoral College.

In the general election, the presidential candidate who wins the popular vote in a state (receives the most votes from citizens), wins all of that state's electors.[¶] Whoever gets a majority of the country's 538 electoral votes, or at least 270, is elected president.[#]

The Electoral College never meets as one body. After Election Day, the electors for the winning presidential candidate in each state gather in their respective statehouses on the same day in December to cast their electoral votes. On January 6 in Washington, D.C., the current vice president presides at a joint session of the new U.S. Congress to tabulate the electoral votes from all the states and formally name the winner, or president-elect.

This method of electing presidents is in harmony with the principle of federalism established by the Framers; the nation is a union of states. Such a system encourages the candidates to seek support over a broader area of the country and not just in the most populous states, counties, and cities,[▲] but it has on occasion resulted in the election of a president who did not receive the most votes of the people nationwide.[◊] This occurred in 2000, but the main controversy in that race was the vote counting in Florida and the number of ballots that could not be counted for either candidate because voters had not completed them properly.

The tally of valid Florida ballots showed the Republican nominee, Texas governor George W. Bush, as the winner, but his Democrat opponent demanded a recount. Bush filed suit in the U.S. Supreme Court, and its ruling, more than a month after Election Day, halted the recounts. Florida's secretary of state certified the election results, which showed Bush as the winner of the state's popular vote by just 537 ballots. That was enough to give him all of Florida's electoral votes and put him over the 270 needed to win the presidency. More than 105 million votes had been cast nationwide.

George W. Bush was inaugurated as the 43rd president. His father had been the 41st. The only other father-son presidents were John Adams (the 2nd) and John Quincy Adams (the 6th). Benjamin Harrison, the 23rd president, was the grandson of the 9th president, William Henry Harrison.

* *Members of the military and others temporarily away from home have long been allowed to vote early using absentee ballots. It is now common in most states for all voters to have the option of casting their ballot by mail or in person over a set period of time before Election Day. Early voting has risen rapidly in recent decades. In 1992, only 7% of voting was done early. In 2024, 65% of all ballots were cast before Election Day.*

† *Since the 1970s, the Iowa caucuses have been the first battleground in the presidential nomination process.*

‡ *Article II of the Constitution requires the president to take the following oath: "I do solemnly swear (or affirm) that I will faithfully execute the Office of President of the United States, and will to the best of my ability, preserve, protect and defend the Constitution of the United States." The words "So help me God" are usually added at the end. The Constitution also requires senators, representatives, and executive and judicial officers at the federal and state level to swear to support the Constitution. Members of the armed forces take an oath to defend the Constitution.*

Though not mandated by the Constitution, immigrants must take the following oath to become citizens: "I hereby declare, on oath, that I absolutely and entirely renounce and abjure all allegiance and fidelity to any foreign prince, potentate, state, or sovereignty, of whom or which I have heretofore been a subject or citizen; that I will support and defend the Constitution and laws of the United States of America against all enemies, foreign and domestic; that I will bear true faith and allegiance to the same; that I will bear arms on behalf of the United States when required by the law ... so help me God."

In a variety of settings, including in schools and at government and civic meetings, citizens face the American flag (also known as Old Glory or the Stars and Stripes) and, with the right hand over the heart, recite the Pledge of Allegiance.

§ *The Constitution prohibits members of Congress or other federal officials from being electors but otherwise leaves it up to each state legislature to decide how its electors are chosen every four years. Presidential electors are selected by state political parties either in primaries, party conventions, or party committees.*

¶ *Maine and Nebraska are exceptions to the winner-take-all norm. They are the only states that allocate electoral votes between presidential candidates.*

If no candidate receives a majority of electoral votes, the 12th Amendment to the Constitution gives the incoming House of Representatives the responsibility of choosing the president from among the three candidates who received the most electoral votes. Each state delegation gets one vote. Since ratification of that amendment in 1804, the House of Representatives has decided the presidential election only once, in 1824, when John Quincy Adams was elected even though he did not get the most electoral votes or win the nationwide popular vote.

▲ *New York City's population (8.5 million) is greater than that of 38 states. Los Angeles County's population (9.8 million) is greater than that of 40 states.*

◊ *Five presidents have won in the Electoral College without winning the nationwide popular vote. Eighteen presidents have won the popular vote with only a plurality (not a majority) of the total votes cast nationally.*

75

9/11 and the WAR ON TERROR

On the morning of September 11, 2001, nineteen suicidal terrorists commandeered four American jetliners. They flew two of the planes into the twin towers of the World Trade Center in New York City and crashed a third jet into the Pentagon, the headquarters of the Department of War in Washington, D.C. The fourth airliner was believed to be heading for the White House or the Capitol building when it went down in a Pennsylvania field as passengers fought the terrorists for control of the aircraft. The coordinated operation killed 2,977 people, including 412 firefighters, police officers, and paramedics trying to rescue victims at the World Trade Center when the gigantic skyscrapers collapsed.*

President Bush vowed to find out who was behind the attacks and bring them to justice. He laid out a comprehensive plan for fighting terrorism globally. The United States would enlist the help of other countries in a new kind of war against the terrorists themselves and any government or organization supporting them. Mass surveillance in the U.S. and abroad was a key part of the plan.

Airports tightened security. Congress created a new cabinet-level federal agency, the Department of Homeland Security. State and local governments prepared for and worked to prevent terrorist attacks at their respective levels. Authorities urged citizens to be on the lookout for possible threats and report suspicious activity.

U.S. intelligence agencies soon discovered that the hijackers were members of al-Qaeda, an Islamic terrorist organization led by Osama bin Laden. The Taliban government in Afghanistan supported bin Laden's activities and had allowed him to set up his headquarters there.

Less than a month after 9/11, the U.S. and the United Kingdom (U.K., or Britain), along with some 30 other nations, invaded Afghanistan. The military coalition drove the Taliban regime from power and destroyed the main al-Qaeda camps, but elements of both organizations remained in the country, and bin Laden evaded capture. In spite of the ongoing war, Afghans held elections, and a new representative government began the process of rebuilding the country with support from coalition nations.

The Bush administration regarded Iraq as the next most dangerous threat in the war on terror. The country was a haven for terrorists and a sponsor of terrorist acts though not implicated in the 9/11 attacks.

The formal ceasefire in the 1991 Gulf War went into effect only after Iraq agreed to restrictions on its military capability. For years, Iraq's president, Saddam Hussein, thwarted United Nations inspectors trying to verify his government's compliance. Intelligence sources in 2003 believed he possessed or was in the process of acquiring chemical, biological, or nuclear weapons, commonly referred to as weapons of mass destruction (WMD).

After Iraq failed to fully respond to diplomatic efforts to resolve the impasse, the United States, with help from the U.K. and other nations, invaded Iraq. Coalition forces quickly defeated the Iraqi military and toppled the government but did not find the suspected WMD.

Most Iraqis welcomed the downfall of the brutal Hussein regime. Securing the peace proved to be much more difficult. Terrorists from other countries joined Iraqi insurgents in disrupting and killing coalition troops and Iraqi citizens trying to establish a free society after decades under a dictatorship.

Despite the instability caused by the lack of security, the Iraqi people ratified a constitution and elected representatives to a new government. They created a tribunal to try members of the old guard for their crimes. Saddam Hussein was hanged after a lengthy trial.

* *The destruction in New York was such that 1,100 victims have never been forensically identified.*

76
FINANCIAL CRISIS

Low interest rates, relaxed qualifications for home loans, and rapidly appreciating real estate values contributed to a surge in construction, home sales, and financing beginning around 1998. But borrowers took on too much debt, including cash loans using the appreciated equity in their homes as collateral. Banks and other lenders, in some instances under pressure from federal agencies and community organizations, made "subprime" mortgage loans to home buyers whose credit worthiness did not meet conventional standards. Speculation in investment properties and vacation homes was rampant. Primary residences accounted for only 60 percent of purchases in 2005, a record low.

In 2006, the supply of available housing far exceeded the demand, causing prices to plummet. The value of millions of homes, including those not for sale, fell below what was owed on them. When those homeowners stopped paying their mortgages, lenders took possession of the distressed properties. Banks and other firms with substantial holdings in "toxic" mortgage-related assets incurred huge losses, scaled back their lending, and saw precipitous declines in their stock prices and cash reserves. With the country sliding into a recession brought on by the housing and mortgage meltdown, the federal government intervened to stimulate the economy and bail out certain businesses deemed "too large to fail."

Fannie Mae and Freddie Mac, two government-sponsored enterprises created decades earlier to facilitate home ownership, owned or guaranteed half of the $12 trillion in mortgages in the United States, but they were buckling under the weight of bad subprime mortgages they had taken on. Worried that bankruptcies of that magnitude might cripple the nation's financial system, the federal government took over the two publicly traded corporations in September 2008.

The largest bankruptcy in history occurred that same month when the Wall Street financial services firm of Lehman Brothers went under due to its stake in subprime mortgages. The collapse of Washington Mutual followed, the largest U.S. bank failure ever. Congress legislated more than $1 trillion to address the financial turmoil.

77
OBAMA, HEALTH CARE, ENERGY, and BIN LADEN

In the midst of the economic downturn, America reached a milestone in 2008 when Illinois Senator Barack Obama, a Democrat, was elected as the first African-American president of the United States. He achieved his chief policy goal by signing a bill that brought major regulatory reform to medical care. It made health insurance available to everyone while imposing financial penalties on those refusing coverage. Enforcement was by the IRS. The legislation was projected to cost at least a trillion dollars.

Technological advances led to a boom in energy. The U.S. strengthened its world dominance in natural gas thanks to production doubling in Louisiana and increasing tenfold in Pennsylvania. Crude oil production surged in Texas and North Dakota, catapulting America past Saudi Arabia and Russia in petroleum output.

After a 10-year manhunt, U.S. intelligence agencies located Osama bin Laden's hideout in Pakistan in 2011. President Obama ordered elite Navy commandos to storm the compound. They killed the terrorist mastermind then flew by helicopter to a U.S. aircraft carrier and buried the body at sea.

The United States military pulled out of Iraq later that year but returned in 2014 when the Iraqi military was unable to stop an al-Qaeda offshoot, the Islamic State of Iraq and Syria (ISIS), from taking over a large part of Iraq. The war and its aftermath cost the lives of 4,600 U.S. servicemembers and left another 32,600 wounded.

In Afghanistan, U.S. combat operations officially ended in 2014, but, unlike in Iraq, it was not followed by a complete pullout. A residual force remained, mostly in an advisory and training role. That war claimed the lives of 2,500 American troops; 20,800 were wounded.

Later in his second term, Obama restored diplomatic relations with Cuba and granted legal status and work visas to millions of people living in the U.S. illegally. He also lifted economic sanctions on Iran after that Islamic state agreed to inspections and limits to its nuclear program.

78
TRUMP, LOCKDOWN, and ELECTION INTEGRITY

In 2016, Democrat Hillary Clinton, a former secretary of state, U.S. senator from New York, and first lady, became the first woman to win the presidential nomination of a major political party. The Republican nominee, also from New York, was unique as well. Donald Trump was a billionaire business owner, TV celebrity, and political novice. His victory in the general election, propelled by his campaign slogans "Make America Great Again" (MAGA) and "America First," stunned the political establishment.*

President Trump's economic plan included comprehensive tax reform, fewer government regulations, and foreign trade deals more advantageous to the United States than in the past. The growing economy led to a drop in the unemployment rate to 3.5 percent, a 50-year low. American companies with international operations moved more than $1 trillion in profits back to the U.S. The president opened up 1½ million acres in Alaska for oil and gas drilling as the U.S. became a net exporter of energy for the first time in nearly 70 years. Along the border with Mexico, he began building a wall to curtail illegal entries.

Trump made history as the first American president to meet with the leader of North Korea or set foot in that hostile country. The focus of the summits was the denuclearization of the Korean peninsula. The president reimposed economic sanctions on Iran and withdrew from the Reagan-era Intermediate-range Nuclear Forces (INF) Treaty after Russia violated its terms. He signed legislation creating a sixth branch of the military, the Space Force, which will operate as a component of the Air Force, much like the Marine Corps is a branch within the Department of the Navy.†

The White House garnered broad support for a sweeping criminal justice reform bill that reduced sentences for certain federal crimes, placed inmates in prisons closer to their families, and helped convicts become productive law-abiding citizens after their incarceration.

In December of 2019, the House of Representatives impeached President Trump over his request that Ukraine investigate possible corruption in that country involving Obama's vice president, Joe Biden, who had entered the race as a candidate to unseat Trump in the 2020 election. The Senate acquitted the president, and he continued to serve.

A virus, Covid-19, that originated in China in December of 2019 quickly spread across the globe and caused major disruptions in economic, social, and religious activity. Nearly everyone in the U.S. complied with some form of quarantine. Twenty-two million Americans lost their livelihoods when businesses shut down, in many cases under orders from local and state officials. To assist struggling workers, businesses, and state and local governments, the federal government passed a $2 trillion aid bill.

The Trump administration partnered with medical companies to produce vaccines, therapeutics, and diagnostics in record time, just months instead of years. But by the end of 2020, more than 350,000 Americans who contracted Covid-19 had died. The virus was the sole cause of death, however, in only six percent of the cases, according to the Centers for Disease Control (CDC).

The pandemic was the backdrop for unprecedented changes in the way the 2020 election was conducted. Local governments accepted millions of dollars from private entities to fund election administration, including money for unsupervised outdoor drop boxes for casting mail-in ballots. According to the Census Bureau, 38 million more mail-in votes were counted in 2020 than in 2016. These and other anomalies, particularly in the most populous counties in Pennsylvania, Michigan, Wisconsin, Georgia, and Arizona, raised questions about the integrity of the results, especially in the presidential race. Vote counting continued for days after Election Day before Biden was pronounced the winner with 81 million votes, 15 million (23%) more than Obama or Hillary Clinton had received in recent elections.

On January 6, the day a joint session of Congress was scheduled to formally count the electoral votes from the states, tens of thousands of President Trump's supporters gathered on the mall in Washington, D.C. to protest what they regarded as a fraudulent election. Some in the group breached police barricades and entered the Capitol, forcing members of Congress to evacuate. In the melee, a Capitol police officer shot and killed one of the protesters. When order was restored, the delegates reconvened and certified the electoral vote victory for 78-year-old Joe Biden, the oldest president in American history.

* *President Trump, like Herbert Hoover and John Kennedy, donated his entire presidential salary. The current compensation, set by Congress, is $400,000 per year. Presidents from Washington to Grant (the 18th) received $25,000 annually. Members of Congress currently receive $174,000 per year plus travel allowances and housing subsidies.*

† *The Coast Guard, currently part of Homeland Security, can be transferred to the Navy (and thus the War Department), as was done in World Wars I and II. Each state*

has its own military force, the National Guard (Army and Air Force only), made up mostly of part-time troops who usually deploy only within their state under the direction of the governor. When the need arises during foreign conflicts or national emergencies, however, they may be deployed full-time with the regular armed forces of the United States under the direction of the president.

79
AFGHANISTAN WITHDRAWAL and TRUMP RETURN

After President Biden announced the withdrawal of all U.S. troops from Afghanistan in 2021, the Taliban quickly defeated the Afghan army and overthrew the elected government. During the chaotic evacuation of Americans as well as Afghans who had assisted the United States over the previous 20 years, 13 U.S. service members were killed by a suicide bomber. Some American citizens were left stranded, and billions of dollars in U.S. military equipment, much of it technologically advanced, fell into the hands of the new Islamic state.

In 2024, Biden and former president Trump won their respective party primaries, thus setting up a rematch in the presidential election, but after a poor debate performance, Biden dropped out of the race, and his vice president became the Democrat nominee. Meanwhile, Trump was nearly killed at a campaign rally when an assassin's bullet struck him in the ear. Secret Service failures at the event led to congressional investigations.

On Election Day, Donald Trump capped off his political comeback by winning 312 electoral votes as well as the nationwide popular vote. The victory made him only the second president in U.S. history elected to non-consecutive terms.* Upon taking office again, President Trump, the nation's 45th and 47th chief executive, immediately began implementing his agenda, which included securing the border, deporting illegal immigrants, and designating Mexican drug cartels and violent gangs from other countries as terrorists.† He imposed or raised tariffs on products from countries that restricted the importation of U.S. products,‡ and he created a commission to discover the root causes of the declining mental and physical health of Americans, especially children.

To streamline the bureaucracy, uncover corruption, eliminate unnecessary and unauthorized expenditures, and downsize the federal workforce of 2.3 million civilian employees, the president established the Department of Government Efficiency (DOGE). He also signed an executive order to evaluate the security of electronic voting, make Election Day the deadline for receiving ballots, require voters to provide documentary identification, and prohibit non-citizens from voting or being otherwise involved in federal elections.

In June of 2025, in the midst of an armed conflict between Israel and Iran, President Trump ordered an attack on Iran's nuclear facilities using U.S. stealth bombers and submarine-launched cruise missiles to prevent that country's terrorist regime from developing a nuclear weapon.

* *Grover Cleveland, the 22nd and 24th president, served from 1885 to 1889 and from 1893 to 1897.*

† *The Center for Immigration Studies estimated that the illegal immigrant population in the U.S. declined by 1.6 million in the first six months of 2025, to 14.2 million.*

‡ *Taxation is the constitutional purview of the legislative branch, but, recognizing the need for a president to have greater flexibility during national emergencies or unfair international trade situations, Congress passed legislation in 1930, 1962, 1974, and 1977 to delegate some of its tariff authority to the president. The exercising of that statutory authority is subject to congressional or judicial review.*

THE ROAD AHEAD

On July 1, 1776, as the Second Continental Congress struggled to decide whether to declare independence, John Adams rose from his seat and addressed his fellow delegates for two hours without notes in one of the greatest speeches in American history. He said, "We are in the very midst of revolution, the most complete, unexpected, and remarkable of any in the history of the world. How few of the human race have ever had an opportunity of choosing a system of government for themselves and their children ... While I live, let me have a country, a free country."

The United States has been a beacon of freedom since its founding and became, in less than 200 years, the wealthiest and most powerful nation in the world. That story is the common heritage of every citizen. An understanding of history gives us a better perspective with which to view current events, solve the problems of our day, and plan ahead. Patrick Henry said, "I know of no way of judging the future but by the past." You now have a solid foundation from which to judge.

Much of what we value as Americans we owe to the Constitution and the delegates in Philadelphia who created it. No one had more intimate knowledge of their deliberations than James Madison, who wrote:

> Whatever may be the judgment pronounced on the competency of the architects of the Constitution, or whatever may be the destiny of the edifice prepared by them, I feel it a duty to express my profound and solemn conviction ... that there never was an assembly of men, charged with a great and arduous trust, who were more pure in their motives, or more exclusively or anxiously devoted to the object committed to them, than were the members of the Federal Convention of 1787, to the object of devising and proposing a constitutional system which would ... best secure the permanent liberty and happiness of their country.

After the Constitutional Convention adjourned, citizens were anxious to know what had been decided. A woman came up to Benjamin Franklin and asked, "Well, Doctor, what have we got, a republic or a monarchy?" He replied, "A republic, if you can keep it." Each of us plays a role in determining the rest of our history and what kind of world we will pass down. By responding positively to that challenge, we will help preserve what George Washington said was "the brightest morn that ever dawned upon any country," and we will show our gratitude for the extraordinary legacy we have inherited as citizens of the United States of America.

Selected Bibliography

Ambrose, Stephen E. *Undaunted Courage: Meriwether Lewis, Thomas Jefferson, and the Opening of the American West*. New York: Simon & Schuster, 1996.

Bennett, Lerone. *Before the Mayflower: A History of Black America*. New York: Penguin Books, 1993.

Boyer, Paul S., et al., eds. *The Oxford Companion to United States History*. New York: Oxford University Press, 2001.

Davis, William C. *Look Away! A History of the Confederate States of America*. New York: Simon & Schuster, 2002.

Eltis, David. *The Trans-Atlantic Slave Trade Database*. Emory University. Web. 2025.

Farrand, Max. *The Framing of the Constitution of the United States*. New Haven: Yale University Press, 1976.

Foner, Eric. *Reconstruction: America's Unfinished Revolution, 1863-1877*. New York: Harper & Row, 1988.

Heinrichs, Waldo. *Threshold of War: Franklin D. Roosevelt & American Entry into World War II*. New York: Oxford University Press, 1988.

Keegan, John. *The First World War*. New York: A. Knopf, 1999.

Ketchum, Richard M. *The Winter Soldiers*. Garden City, NY: Doubleday & Co., 1973.

Langguth, A.J. *Patriots: The Men Who Started the American Revolution*. New York: Simon & Schuster, 1988.

Leckie, Robert. *From Sea to Shining Sea: From the War of 1812 to the Mexican War, the Saga of America's Expansion*. New York: Harper Collins, 1993.

Morison, Samuel Eliot, and Henry Steele Commager. *The Growth of the American Republic*. New York: Oxford University Press, 1962.

Morris, Richard B., ed. *Encyclopedia of American History*. New York: Harper & Row, 1965.

Nash, Gary B. *Red, White, and Black: The Peoples of Early America*. Englewood Cliffs, New Jersey: Prentice-Hall, 1982.

Schlesinger, Arthur. *The Almanac of American History*. New York: Putnam, 1983.

Taylor, Alan. *American Colonies*, ed. Eric Foner. New York: Penguin, 2002.

Tindall, George Brown, Charles W. Eagles, and David E. Shi. *America: A Narrative History*. New York: Norton, 1999.

U.S. Bureau of the Census. *Historical Statistics of the United States, Colonial Times to 1957*. Washington, D.C., 1961.

Vaughan, Alden T. *American Genesis: Captain John Smith and the Founding of Virginia*. Boston: Little, Brown and Co., 1975.

Key Years and Events

1492 - First voyage of Columbus begins (ends 1493)

1497 - John Cabot's first voyage to North America

1565 - Saint Augustine founded in Florida

1598 - Spaniards begin colonizing the American West north of Mexico

1607 - Jamestown colony founded in Virginia

1620 - Pilgrims settle in Massachusetts at Plymouth

1630 - Puritans establish the Massachusetts Bay Colony in Boston

1732 - Georgia founded, last of the Thirteen Colonies

1754 - French and Indian War begins (ends 1763)

1763 - Royal Proclamation of 1763

1775 - Revolutionary War begins (ends 1783)

1776 - Declaration of Independence, founding of the United States of America

1787 - Constitutional Convention

1789 - Federal government begins functioning under the Constitution with George Washington as president

1791 - Bill of Rights ratified (first 10 amendments to the Constitution)

1797 - John Adams inaugurated as the 2nd chief executive, setting the precedent for peaceful presidential succession

1801 - Thomas Jefferson, a Democrat-Republican, becomes president, succeeding John Adams, a Federalist, setting the precedent for peaceful transfer of power from one political party to another

1803 - Louisiana Purchase

1804 - Lewis & Clark expedition begins (ends 1806)

1808 - Importation of slaves banned

1812 - War of 1812 begins (ends 1815)

1821 - Florida acquired

1830 - Indian Removal Act

1845 - Republic of Texas acquired

1846 - Mexican War begins (ends 1848); Oregon Territory acquired

1848 - Mexican Cession

1861 - Civil War begins (ends 1865)

1863 - Emancipation Proclamation

1865 - President Lincoln assassinated; Postwar Reconstruction begins

1867 - Alaska purchased from Russia

1869 - First transcontinental railroad completed

1872 Yellowstone established, first national park in the world

1898 - Hawaii annexed; Spanish-American War, Puerto Rico & Guam acquired

1909 - Corporate income tax instituted

1913 - Personal income tax permanently established; Federal Reserve created; 17th Amendment ratified to elect senators by popular vote

1917 - U.S. enters World War I (ends 1918)

1918 - Flu pandemic (ends 1919)

1920 - Women secure the constitutional right to vote nationwide

1929 - Great Depression begins (lasts a decade)

1941 - Pearl Harbor attacked; U.S. enters World War II (ends 1945)
1945 - Atom bombs dropped on Japan; United Nations created
1950 - Korean War begins (armistice 1953)
1956 - Construction begins on interstate road system
1962 - Cuban missile crisis
1963 - President Kennedy assassinated
1964 - Gulf of Tonkin incident, Vietnam War escalation
1965 - Great Society legislation, pivotal immigration law
1969 - Astronauts Neil Armstrong and Buzz Aldrin walk on the moon
1971 - 26th Amendment sets the minimum voting age at 18
1972 - Military service becomes voluntary
1974 - President Nixon resigns
1979 - Iran seizes U.S. embassy in Tehran (hostage crisis ends 1981)
1987 - President Reagan signs landmark arms control treaty with Russia
1991 - Gulf War
2001 - 9/11 attacks; Afghan War begins (ends 2014)
2003 - Iraq War begins (ends 2011)
2008 - Barack Obama elected president, first African-American
2016 - Donald Trump, billionaire and political novice, elected president
2020 - Global pandemic and unprecedented lockdown of the U.S.
2024 - President Trump re-elected to non-consecutive term

Calendar Dates to Remember

January 15 (1929)	- Birthday of Martin Luther King Jr. (observed 3rd Monday in January)
February 22 (1732)	- George Washington's Birthday (observed 3rd Monday in February)
April 15	- Tax Day (individual income tax returns due)
April 19 (1775)	- Revolutionary War began near Boston
May (last Monday)	- Memorial Day (to honor all who died in military service)
June 6 (1944)	- D-Day/Normandy Invasion
July 4 (1776)	- Independence Day (Declaration of Independence adopted and United States of America founded)
September 11 (2001)	- 9/11 terrorist attacks
September 17 (1787)	- Constitution Day (Constitution signed)
October 12 (1492)	- Columbus Day (to commemorate the explorer's landfall in the New World; observed 2nd Monday in October)
November (various)	- Election Day (1st Tuesday after 1st Monday, even years)
November 11	- Veterans Day (to honor all who served in the military)
December 7 (1941)	- Pearl Harbor Day (to remember Americans killed in the Japanese attack)

States in Alphabetical Order

State	Congressional Districts	Capital	Admitted	Nickname
Alabama	7	Montgomery	1819 (22nd)	Heart of Dixie
Alaska	1	Juneau	1959 (49th)	The Last Frontier
Arizona	9	Phoenix	1912 (48th)	Grand Canyon State
Arkansas	4	Little Rock	1836 (25th)	Natural State
California	52	Sacramento	1850 (31st)	Golden State
Colorado	8	Denver	1876 (38th)	Centennial State
Connecticut	5	Hartford	1788 (5th)	Constitution State
Delaware	1	Dover	1787 (1st)	First State
Florida	28	Tallahassee	1845 (27th)	Sunshine State
Georgia	14	Atlanta	1788 (4th)	Peach State
Hawaii	2	Honolulu	1959 (50th)	Aloha State
Idaho	2	Boise	1890 (43rd)	Gem State
Illinois	17	Springfield	1818 (21st)	Prairie State
Indiana	9	Indianapolis	1816 (19th)	Hoosier State
Iowa	4	Des Moines	1846 (29th)	Hawkeye State
Kansas	4	Topeka	1861 (34th)	Sunflower State
Kentucky	6	Frankfort	1792 (15th)	Bluegrass State
Louisiana	6	Baton Rouge	1812 (18th)	Pelican State
Maine	2	Augusta	1820 (23rd)	Pine Tree State
Maryland	8	Annapolis	1788 (7th)	Old Line State
Massachusetts	9	Boston	1788 (6th)	Bay State
Michigan	13	Lansing	1837 (26th)	Wolverine State
Minnesota	8	Saint Paul	1858 (32nd)	North Star State
Mississippi	4	Jackson	1817 (20th)	Magnolia State
Missouri	8	Jefferson City	1821 (24th)	Show Me State
Montana	2	Helena	1889 (41st)	Treasure State
Nebraska	3	Lincoln	1867 (37th)	Cornhusker State
Nevada	4	Carson City	1864 (36th)	Silver State
New Hampshire	2	Concord	1788 (9th)	Granite State
New Jersey	12	Trenton	1787 (3rd)	Garden State
New Mexico	3	Santa Fe	1912 (47th)	Land of Enchantment
New York	26	Albany	1788 (11th)	Empire State
North Carolina	14	Raleigh	1789 (12th)	Tarheel State
North Dakota	1	Bismarck	1889 (39th)	Peace Garden State
Ohio	15	Columbus	1803 (17th)	Buckeye State
Oklahoma	5	Oklahoma City	1907 (46th)	Sooner State
Oregon	6	Salem	1859 (33rd)	Beaver State
Pennsylvania	17	Harrisburg	1787 (2nd)	Keystone State
Rhode Island	2	Providence	1790 (13th)	Ocean State
South Carolina	7	Columbia	1788 (8th)	Palmetto State
South Dakota	1	Pierre	1889 (40th)	Mount Rushmore State
Tennessee	9	Nashville	1796 (16th)	Volunteer State
Texas	38	Austin	1845 (28th)	Lone Star State
Utah	4	Salt Lake City	1896 (45th)	Beehive State
Vermont	1	Montpelier	1791 (14th)	Green Mountain State
Virginia	11	Richmond	1788 (10th)	Old Dominion
Washington	10	Olympia	1889 (42nd)	Evergreen State
West Virginia	2	Charleston	1863 (35th)	Mountain State
Wisconsin	8	Madison	1848 (30th)	Badger State
Wyoming	1	Cheyenne	1890 (44th)	Equality State
	435			

Presidents of the United States

No.	Name	Years in Office	Party	Age Taking Office	Home State	Lifespan
1	George Washington	1789-97	n/a	57	VA	1732-1799
2	John Adams	1797-01	Federalist	61	MA	1735-1826
3	Thomas Jefferson	1801-09	Dem-Repub	57	VA	1743-1826
4	James Madison	1809-17	Dem-Repub	57	VA	1751-1836
5	James Monroe	1817-25	Dem-Repub	58	VA	1758-1831
6	John Quincy Adams	1825-29	Dem-Repub	57	MA	1767-1848
7	Andrew Jackson	1829-37	Democrat	61	TN	1767-1845
8	Martin Van Buren	1837-41	Democrat	54	NY	1782-1862
9	William Harrison	1841	Whig	68	OH	1773-1841
10	John Tyler	1841-45	Whig	51	VA	1790-1862
11	James K. Polk	1845-49	Democrat	49	TN	1795-1849
12	Zachary Taylor	1849-50	Whig	64	KY	1784-1850
13	Millard Fillmore	1850-53	Whig	50	NY	1800-1874
14	Franklin Pierce	1853-57	Democrat	48	NH	1804-1869
15	James Buchanan	1857-61	Democrat	65	PA	1791-1868
16	Abraham Lincoln	1861-65	Republican	52	IL	1809-1865
17	Andrew Johnson	1865-69	Democrat	56	TN	1808-1875
18	Ulysses S. Grant	1869-77	Republican	46	IL	1822-1885
19	Rutherford B. Hayes	1877-81	Republican	54	OH	1822-1893
20	James A. Garfield	1881	Republican	49	OH	1831-1881
21	Chester A. Arthur	1881-85	Republican	51	NY	1829-1886
22	Grover Cleveland	1885-89	Democrat	47	NY	1837-1908
23	Benjamin Harrison	1889-93	Republican	55	IN	1833-1901
24	Grover Cleveland	1893-97	Democrat	55	NY	1837-1908
25	William McKinley	1897-01	Republican	54	OH	1843-1901
26	Theodore Roosevelt	1901-09	Republican	42	NY	1858-1919
27	William Howard Taft	1909-13	Republican	51	OH	1857-1930
28	Woodrow Wilson	1913-21	Democrat	56	NJ	1856-1924
29	Warren G. Harding	1921-23	Republican	55	OH	1865-1923
30	Calvin Coolidge	1923-29	Republican	51	MA	1872-1933
31	Herbert Hoover	1929-33	Republican	54	CA	1874-1964
32	Franklin D. Roosevelt	1933-45	Democrat	51	NY	1882-1945
33	Harry S. Truman	1945-53	Democrat	60	MO	1884-1972
34	Dwight D. Eisenhower	1953-61	Republican	62	KS	1890-1969
35	John F. Kennedy	1961-63	Democrat	43	MA	1917-1963
36	Lyndon B. Johnson	1963-69	Democrat	55	TX	1908-1973
37	Richard M. Nixon	1969-74	Republican	56	CA	1913-1994
38	Gerald R. Ford	1974-77	Republican	61	MI	1913-2006
39	Jimmy Carter	1977-81	Democrat	52	GA	1924-2024
40	Ronald Reagan	1981-89	Republican	69	CA	1911-2004
41	George H.W. Bush	1989-93	Republican	64	TX	1924-2018
42	Bill Clinton	1993-01	Democrat	46	AR	1946-
43	George W. Bush	2001-09	Republican	54	TX	1946-
44	Barack Obama	2009-17	Democrat	47	IL	1961-
45	Donald J. Trump	2017-21	Republican	70	NY	1946-
46	Joe Biden	2021-25	Democrat	78	DE	1942-
47	Donald J. Trump	2025-	Republican	78	NY	1946-

Great Seal of the United States (original design 1782)

front

- The eagle symbolizes the nation's strength.
- Breaking through the cloud above the eagle's head is a new constellation of 13 stars symbolizing the original states.
- *E Pluribus Unum*, the 13-letter Latin phrase written on the ribbon in the eagle's beak, means "out of many, one" – i.e., the states united as one nation.
- The shield on the eagle's breast is held in place without outside support, signifying the nation's self-reliance. The solid top of the shield (the national government) unites and is supported by the 13 pillars (states) underneath.
- In one set of talons, the eagle holds a symbol of peace: an olive branch with 13 leaves and 13 olives. In the other talons are 13 arrows signifying the power to make war. The eagle's head is turned toward the olive branch to denote the country's preference for peace.

back

- The 13-layer pyramid symbolizes the nation's strength and permanence, but the structure is unfinished. The year 1776 is written in Roman numerals at the base.
- The eye symbolizes God, and *Annuit Coeptis*, the 13-letter Latin phrase at the top, means "He has favored our undertakings."
- *Novus Ordo Seclorum*, the Latin phrase at the bottom, means "A new order of the ages."

The Seven Articles of the U.S. Constitution

Article 1 – Structure and powers of Congress (*Legislative Branch*)

Article 2 – Structure and powers of the President (*Executive Branch*)

Article 3 – Structure and powers of Federal Courts (*Judicial Branch*)

Article 4 – Every state is guaranteed a representative government and protection from invasion and domestic violence.

– Citizens enjoy the same fundamental rights ("privileges and immunities") in all the states and may travel freely throughout the country but not to escape criminal prosecution.

– Court decisions in one state must be honored (given "full faith and credit") in the other states.

– No new state may be created by splitting an existing state or by combining states or parts of states without the approval of Congress and the legislatures of the states concerned.

Article 5 – Process for amending the Constitution

Article 6 – The Constitution, federal laws, and U.S. treaties are the supreme law of the land.

– Legislative, executive, and judicial officers at the federal and state level must take an oath to support the Constitution.

– Religious tests for holding federal office are forbidden.

Article 7 – Ratification of the Constitution by the original 13 states

About the Author

Randolph G. Russell's informative, entertaining, and motivational presentations have resonated with audiences across the country. In addition to his expertise in history, the author is an accomplished musician who has performed in many European countries and throughout the United States. He holds degrees from the University of Miami and the University of Florida.

National Anthem

Image Credits

(The images are distributed under one of four public domain licenses: cc-by-sa 1.0 thru 4.0.)

AC: Architect of the Capitol LOC: Library of Congress MMA: Metropolitan Museum of Art
NA: National Archives NPG: National Portrait Gallery NPS: National Park Service

Statue of Liberty (cover), Zinneke; Second Continental Congress, NPG; U.S. map, U.S. Geological Survey; World map, vector-worldmap.com; Great Seal, U.S. Congress.

Basket, Daderot; Totem pole, Joshua Murdough; Petroglyphs, James St. John; Cliff dwelling, inkknife_2000; Bow and arrow, Hamilton Irving Marlatt; Teepees, Wellcome Images; Blackfoot Indian, LOC; Apache bride, NA; Monks Mound, NA; Mica serpent, Daderot; Canoe, Paul VanDerWerf; Effigy pipe, Tim Evanson; Arrowhead, MMA; Papoose, Missouri History Museum; Wampum, Daderot; Iroquois longhouse, Laslovarga; Columbus, AC; St. Augustine fort, Oliv0; John Smith, DCwom; Pocahontas, NPG; Jamestown, Tony Fischer; *Mayflower*, Jérôme; Pilgrims, New York Historical Society; Boston, Ingfbruno; Anne Hutchinson, Yale University; Fraunces Tavern, Arun De Joe; William Penn, Houston Museum of Fine Arts; Hampton Plantation, Brian Stansberry.

Concord's North Bridge, NPS; Minuteman, Daderot; Thomas Paine, NPG; Thomas Jefferson, Department of State; John Adams, White House; Benjamin Franklin, NPG; Declaration of Independence, NA; General Washington, James Peale; Washington crossing the Delaware, MMA; March to Valley Forge, Museum of the American Revolution; Von Steuben, Pennsylvania State Capitol; British surrender, AC; James Madison, LOC; Alexander Hamilton, National Gallery of Art; Constitutional Convention, AC; Preamble, NA; U.S. Capitol, AC; White House, HiraV; Supreme Court building, Marielam1; Voting booths, Tim Evanson; Arlington, Daniel Zimmermann.

Lewis & Clark, Montana House of Representatives; White House burning, White House Historical Association; Erie Canal, AC; Francis Scott Key, LOC; Mill, Gabor Eszes; Steam locomotive, Centpacrr; Tribal boundaries, Tcr25; Slaves loaded onto ship, unknown origin; Andrew Jackson, National Gallery of Art; Cotton gin, LOC; Slave family, unknown origin; Atlanta slave shop, LOC; Harriet Tubman, NPS; Frederick Douglass, NA; Spirit of the Frontier, LOC; Alamo, Bypassers; Pioneers, C.C.A. Christensen; U.S. troops in Mexico City, The Museum of Fine Arts, Houston; Oregon (Mt. Hood), Sandra Oja; Sutter's Mill, Nick Ares; Miner, L. C. McClure; James K. Polk, LOC.

Harriet Beecher Stowe, NPG; Underground Railroad, Cincinnati Art Museum; Dred Scott, unknown origin; John Brown, LOC; Abraham Lincoln, Mead Art Museum; Fort Sumter, LOC; Blockade runner, LOC; Ulysses S. Grant, LOC; Jefferson Davis, LOC; Robert E. Lee, MMA; U.S. flag, Jacobolus; Confederate White House, Virginia Commonwealth University Libraries; Confederate battle flag, Hugh Talman (Smithsonian Institution); Ironclads, LOC; Antietam, unknown origin; President Lincoln with troops, LOC; Clara Barton, NA; Emancipation Proclamation, LOC; Pickett's Charge, Pennsylvania State Archives; March to the Sea, LOC; Appomattox, NPS; Richmond, MMA; Lincoln assassination, Adam Cuerden; Andrew Johnson, LOC; Hiram Revels, LOC; Ku Klux Klan, Associated Press; Former adversaries, LOC.

Andrew Carnegie, LOC; Steel mill, LOC; Carnegie library, S.H. Kress & Co.; John D. Rockefeller, NPG; Oil wells, NA; J.P. Morgan, LOC; Emma Lazarus, New York Historical Society; Thomas Edison, NPS; Alexander Graham Bell, LOC; Strike violence, Harper's Weekly; Immigrant ship, LOC; Urban traffic, New York Times; Tenement, Missouri History Museum; Howard University law graduates, LOC; Medical students, Women's Medical College of Pennsylvania; Transcontinental railroad, Andrew J. Russell; Little Bighorn, LOC; Sitting Bull, D.F. Barry; Bison skulls, Soerfm; Yellowstone buffalo, NPS/Jacob W. Frank; Old Faithful, NPS/Diane Renkin; Cowboy, unknown origin; Barbed wire, Sean McGrath; Homestead, NPS; USS *Maine*, University of Toronto; Rough Riders, LOC; Baseball, unknown origin; Alaska, NA; Hawaii, LOC; Panama Canal, LOC.

Wright Flyer, LOC; Ford Model T, unknown origin; Silent movie, United Artists; Radio, Joe Haupt; Snake oil, Jim Griffin; Child labor, LOC; IRS logo, Department of the Treasury; Uncle Sam, LOC; Gas masks, NA; Trench warfare, LOC; Flu epidemic, National Museum of Health and Medicine; Prohibition, LOC; Suffragists, New York Times; Art Deco, Rambhai mb; Fashion, LOC; Charles Lindbergh, LOC; Bessie Smith, LOC; Duke Ellington, unknown origin; Great Depression relocation, Durova; Unemployed, NA; Franklin D. Roosevelt, NA; Plains dust storm, NOAA; Social Security, NA; Hoover Dam, Mariordo; Pearl Harbor, NA; Women building aircraft, LOC; Normandy Invasion, NA; Concentration camp, NA; Air power, U.S. Air Force; Sea power, NA; Iwo Jima, Alexis Jazz; Atom bomb, NA; V-J Day, Ed Westcott; Marshall Plan, NA.

Berlin Airlift, U.S. Air Force; Chosin Reservoir, Peter McDonald; Television, NA; Polio vaccination, Mississippi Department of Archives and History; Elvis, Metro-Goldwyn-Mayer; Nuclear plant, Historic American Engineering Record; Cuban missile crisis, U.S. Navy; Submarine, U.S. Navy; Nuclear missile silo, Zcobb99; Martin Luther King Jr, U.S. Marine Corps; President Kennedy motorcade, LOC; Johnson swearing-in, JFK Presidential Library; EBT cards, Department of Agriculture; Vietnam War, U.S. Army; Thurgood Marshall, LOC; D.C. riots, LOC; College protests, State Archives of Florida; Drugs, U.S. Army; Woodstock, James M. Shelley; Moon landing, Soerfm; Manatee, U.S. Fish & Wildlife Service; Abortion, Lorie Shaull; Nixon resignation, NA; South Vietnamese, U.S. Marines; President Carter, CIA; U.S. embassy in Tehran, unknown origin; President Reagan, NA; Sandra Day O'Connor, Supreme Court; Personal computer, zeitfaenger.at; Gulf War, U.S. Air Force; 9/11, NPS; Iraq War, U.S. Marines; President Obama, Pete Souza; Situation Room, Pete Souza; President Trump, Shealah Craighead; Border wall, U.S. Customs & Border Protection; Pandemic, Department of Labor; Ballot drop box, SounderBruce; Afghanistan withdrawal, Guilherme Mateus Monteiro; Road Ahead, Sandy Horvath-Dori.

Puerto Rico, LBM1948; Cape Canaveral, Staff Sgt. Jeremy Mosier; Mississippi River, Bridget Coila; French Quarter, Reading Tom; Savannah, Elisa.rolle; Great Smoky Mountains, AppalachianCentrist; Mount Vernon, Mount Vernon Ladies' Association; Smithsonian, David Bjorgen; Vietnam Memorial, Wladia Drummond; Independence Hall, LOC; Assembly Room, Antoine Taveneaux; Liberty Bell, William Zhang; Appalachian Trail, Famartin; Times Square, Terabass; Niagara Falls, Pankaj A; Yale, Ragesoss; Paul Revere, TanRo; Maine, Chandra Hari; Lake Superior, NPS; Mesabi Range, James St. John; Iowa, Lynn Betts; Gateway Arch, Sam Valadi; Mount Rushmore, EGryk; Missouri River, Cmichel67; Air Force Academy, Ahodges7; Monument Valley, Jon Sullivan; Grand Canyon, Antoine Taveneaux; Las Vegas, Clément Bardot; Rhyolite, NoeHill; Death Valley, NA; Hollywood, Adrian104; Sequoias, Tuxyso; Golden Gate, Daniel Schwen; Yosemite, King of Hearts; Glacier National Park, Andrew Parlette; Historical marker, Famartin.

Old San Juan, Puerto Rico

Cape Canaveral

Mississippi River at New Orleans

Slave auction site in French Quarter

Savannah historic district

Great Smoky Mountains

Mount Vernon

Smithsonian Museum

Vietnam Veterans Memorial

Independence Hall

Assembly Room, where the Declaration of Independence and the Constitution were crafted

Liberty Bell

Appalachian Trail

Times Square

Niagara Falls

Yale Law School

Paul Revere & Old North Church

Maine lighthouse

Lake Superior

Surface iron mine in Mesabi Range

Iowa grain harvest

Gateway Arch

Mount Rushmore

Cliffs along the upper Missouri River

Air Force Academy

Monument Valley

Grand Canyon

Las Vegas strip

Rhyolite ghost town

Death Valley desert dunes

Hollywood sign

Giant sequoias

Golden Gate Bridge

Yosemite National Park

Glacier National Park

Historical marker

Made in the USA
Coppell, TX
28 January 2026

70251293R00092